REVISE PEARSON EDEXCEL GCSE (9–1)

Physical Education

MODEL ANSWER WORKBOOK

Series Consultant: Harry Smith

Author: Jennifer Stafford-Brown

Also available to support your revision:

Revise GCSE Study Skills Guide   9781292318875

The **Revise GCSE Study Skills Guide** is full of tried-and-trusted hints and tips for how to learn more effectively. It gives you techniques to help you achieve your best – throughout your GCSE studies and beyond!

Revise GCSE Revision Planner   9781292318868

The **Revise GCSE Revision Planner** helps you to plan and organise your time, step-by-step, throughout your GCSE revision. Use this book and wall chart to mastermind your revision.

For the full range of Pearson revision titles across KS2, KS3, GCSE, Functional Skills, AS/A Level and BTEC visit:
www.pearsonschools.co.uk/revise

Contents

A small bit of small print:
Pearson Edexcel publishes Sample Assessment Material and the Specification on its website. This is the official content and this book should be used in conjunction with it. The questions and mark schemes have been written to help you practise every topic in the book. Remember: the real exam questions and mark schemes may not look like this.

About your exam

Your Pearson Edexcel (9–1) Physical Education GCSE exam comprises two papers.

Paper 1: Fitness and Body Systems

This paper includes the following topics:
Topic 1: Applied anatomy and physiology
Topic 2: Movement analysis
Topic 3: Physical training
Topic 4: Use of data
This paper is…

 1 hour 45 minutes    worth 90 marks   % 36% of the overall qualification

A calculator can be used

Paper 2 Health and Performance

This paper includes the following topics:
Topic 1: Health, fitness and well-being
Topic 2: Sport psychology
Topic 3: Socio-cultural influences
Topic 4: Use of data
This paper is…

 1 hour 15 minutes   90 worth 70 marks   % 24% of the overall qualification

A calculator can be used

Both papers are worth 60% of the final grade and will assess your skills and knowledge using a range of question types:

Closed questions
- Multiple choice

Open questions
- Label the diagram
- complete a table
- Write a short response
- Write an extended response
- Calculate the answer

Pearson Edexcel (9-1) GCSE PE targets all grades from 9 through to 1 and U.

Grades available for this qualification

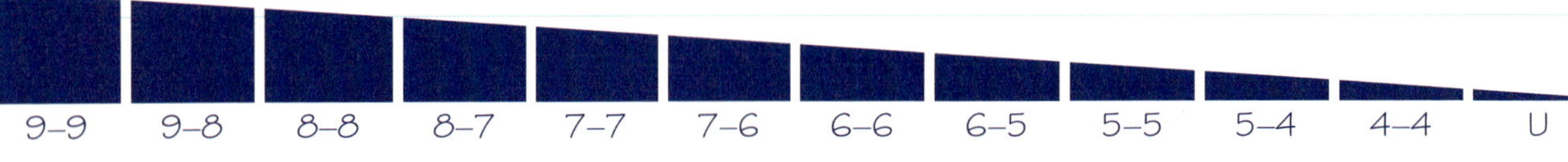

Command words

Assess
Requires reasoned argument of factors to reach a judgement regarding their importance/relevance to the question context. For example 'Assess the relative importance of'

Analyse
Break something down into its component parts, this could be in relation to movement analysis

Classify
Required to group or place on a scale based on characteristics/analysis of characteristics

Complete
Required to add information based on a stimulus/resource. This could be to complete a table, graph, chart or missing word/phrase from a sentence/statement

Describe
Account of something without reasons. Statements in the response need to be linked, for example 'Describe the lever system operating at the elbow'

Calculate
Requires computation in relation to fitness data

Explain
Requires a justification/exemplification of a point. The answer must contain some linked reasoning. For example, the format of the response may be ' fact... because... therefore'

Define
Required to give the meaning or definition of a word/term

Examine
Requires a justification/exemplification of a point based on some analysis or evaluation within the response. For example, 'Examine the role of the first class lever system'

Identify
Can require a selection from a given stimulus or resource, for example an option from a multiple-choice question or analysis of data from source material such as a graph, or can be synonymous with give/state

Evaluate
Review/analyse information, bringing it together to form a conclusion/judgement based on strengths/weaknesses, alternatives, relevant data or information. Come to a supported judgement of a subject's qualities and relation to its context

Discuss
Required to explore the issue/situation/problem that is being assessed in the question context, articulating different or contrasting viewpoints, for example advantages, disadvantages

Justify
Give reasons for answers. This could be a single response to extended writing answers depending on question context. For example, 'Justify the use of interval training to improve'

Give
Generally involves the recall of a fact, or an example based on the given stimulus. For example, 'Give an example of a specific sporting movement....' Can be synonymous with identify/state

Mark schemes

Understanding mark schemes

Mark schemes tell you what the marker is looking for in your answer. Throughout the book, you will be introduced to using mark schemes alongside exam-style answers. Here are some of the things to look out for.

Closed or short answer mark schemes

Your answer doesn't need to match these points word-for-word, but needs to have the same message and use the correct vocabulary.

Question	Answer	Mark
	Knee – max 3 marks There is extension at the knee (1) this is possible because the quadriceps have contracted (1) because the hamstrings which are the antagonistic muscle have relaxed.	3

Each mark aligns with part of the answer, meaning each point is worth one mark.

Extended answer mark schemes

Extended answers are given a level first. Then to award a mark, you need to decide whether the answer is at the top of bottom end of that level.

Question Number	Indicative content	Mark
	• High blood sugar levels indicates diabetes • High levels of sugar in the blood damage blood vessels • If left untreated it can lead to blindness/ kidney damage • Regular exercise helps to regulate insulin levels which have resulted in normal blood sugar levels. • Reduction or no further damage to blood vessels so less likely to suffer from health issues associated with diabetes.	9

The indicative content section is a guide to the sorts of points that would be included in a good answer. The list is not 'exhaustive' which means there may be other correct answers.

Level	Mark	Descriptor
	0	No credit worthy response
Level 1	1–3	Demonstrates isolated elements of knowledge and understanding, with limited technical language used • Limited attempt to apply knowledge to question context • Generic assertions may be presented
Level 2	4–6	Demonstrates mostly accurate knowledge and understanding, with use of appropriate technical language in places • Applies knowledge to question context • Attempts conclusion with support from evidence
Level 3	7–9	Demonstrates accurate knowledge and understanding throughout, including appropriate use of technical language • Applied detailed knowledge to question context throughout • Reaches a valid and well-reasoned conclusion supported by relevant evidence

How to use this book

In this book, you will familiarise yourself with the Pearson Edexcel (9–1) Physical Education GCSE by engaging with exam-style questions, answers and mark schemes. Doing so will mean you know exactly what to expect in the exam and, just as importantly, what will be expected of you.

Each activity type asks you to engage with an exam-style question in a different way. You can work your way from front to back or focus on pages that test the skills you need to improve.

Read the activity instructions carefully before you begin – it's good practice for the exams!

This stamp tells you the level of the student answer on the page. There are three levels of answer: Had a go, Nearly there and Nailed it!

You'll see this stamp on questions that have more than one correct answer. If you're not sure whether your answer is correct, use your Revision Guide or check with your teacher.

Student answers are always written in red.

Hints guide you in the right direction, from advice on tackling the question to guidance on structuring your answer.

In student tips, real-life students share some of their tips and techniques for exam success.

Marker's comments tell you what a student has done well and what could be done better.

Mark schemes tell you what the marker is looking for. See page 2 for more information.

Answers to activities are written in blue. You can find them in the back of the book, starting on page 76. Answers provided in blue will be 'exemplar', which means they're examples of very strong answers.

Complete the answer

1 Complete the student's answer so that it would be awarded 4 marks.

1.1 Muscles work with the skeleton to bring about specific sporting movements.

Complete **Table 1** by:

(a) identifying **two** different muscle fibre types

(b) stating a characteristic of each fibre type. (4)

> **Hint**
> The number of marks available is a good guide to how many points you need to make in your answer. For example, there are 4 marks available here, which generally means that four separate points or items are required in your response.

(a) Muscle fibre type	(b) Characteristic
Type I .... (1)	.... (1)
.... (1)	This fibre is able to contract with very high force. .... (1)

Table 1

> I always follow a fail-safe method when answering exam questions: I read the question, then look at the number of marks available, then read the question again and decide how many points I need to make for each part of the question. This approach really helped me get my timings right in the exam.

2 Complete the student's answer so that it would be awarded 4 marks.

1.2 Blood vessels form part of the cardiovascular system.

Complete **Table 2** by:

(a) stating **one** structure of each blood vessel

(b) stating **one** function of each blood vessel. (4)

Blood vessel	(a) Structure	(b) Function
Vein	Contains valves .... (1)	.... (1)
Artery	.... (1)	Takes blood away from the heart .... (1)

Table 2

Improve the answer

1 Write an improved answer to the question below. Use the hint to make sure your answer achieves the highest possible mark.

1.3 Jackie takes part in a cross-country run.

Table 3 shows Jackie's tidal volume at rest and during her cross-country run.

Tidal volume at rest	500 ml
Tidal volume during cross-country run	800 ml

Table 3

Using the data in **Table 3**, explain the difference in Jackie's tidal volume at rest and during her cross-country run. **(3)**

Had a go

Jackie's tidal volume increases from 500 ml at rest to 800 ml while taking part in a cross-country run. This is because she needs to get more air into her body.

> **Hint**
> This student's answer would gain 1 mark for successfully explaining the difference, but would receive no further marks for explanation. To improve the student's answer, you need to explain why the increase happens, using the correct scientific terms such as 'oxygen' and 'aerobic energy system'. Remember: use the data from the table in your answer.

2 Write an improved answer to the question below. Use the hint to make sure your answer achieves the highest possible mark.

1.4 Alveoli are located in the lungs and are the site of gaseous exchange.

Explain how **one** structure of alveoli aids gaseous exchange. **(2)**

Had a go

Alveoli have semi-permeable membranes and are surrounded by capillaries, which helps with gaseous exchange.

> **Hint**
> In this student's answer, although two structures in the lungs have been identified, the student will gain just 1 mark because the question asks for only one structure to be explained. The student has provided no explanation of how either structure helps with gaseous exchange.

Complete the question

1 Complete the question by adding **two** multiple-choice options. Make sure one is correct.

2.1 (a) Which one of the following correctly states the role of tendons? **(1)**

> **Hint**
> Multiple-choice answers always contain believable answers. Make sure your incorrect option really tests a student's understanding of the role of tendons.

☐ **A** Join bone to bone

☑ **C** ....

☐ **B** Join muscle to muscle

☐ **D** ....

....

2 Complete the question by adding **two** multiple-choice options. Make sure one is correct.

(b) Which one of the following is the correct classification of the neck joint? **(1)**

> **Hint**
> When answering this question, remember that all the multiple-choice options have to name an actual type of joint rather than being made-up terms.

☐ **A** Hinge

☐ **C** Ball and socket

☑ **B** ....

☐ **D** ....

3 Complete the question by adding **two** multiple-choice options.

(c) Which one of the following is **not** a function of the skeleton? **(1)**

> **Hint**
> Watch out! The question asks students to identify which option is incorrect, so you need to write in two **correct** functions of the skeleton.

☐ **A** Protects vital organs

☐ **C** ....

☐ **B** ....

☑ **D** Stores vitamin A

Mark the answer

1 Use the mark scheme below to decide how many marks you would award the student's answer. Give reasons for your decision.

2.2 **Figure 1** shows a person performing a squat using a barbell.

Examine the antagonistic muscle action that takes place at the right knee and right hip as the person rises from the squat position to standing. **(6)**

Figure 1

> **Hint**
> To gain the full 6 marks available for this question, you must use technical terminology in your answer. For example, you should use the term 'extend' rather than 'straighten', and you should name the joints where movement in the leg occurs.

The legs straighten at the knee because the quadriceps have contracted. The other muscles in the antagonistic pair are the hamstrings, and these will relax when the quadriceps muscles contract.

The hip flexes because the gluteus maximus has contracted. The hamstrings are the antagonistic pair and these relax to let the movement happen.

Question	Answer	Mark
2.2	1 mark each for the following linked points. • There is extension at the knee (1). This is possible because the quadriceps have contracted (1) as the hamstrings, which are the antagonistic muscles, have relaxed (1). • There is extension at the hip (1). This is possible because the gluteus maximus has contracted (1) and the hip flexors, which are the antagonistic muscles, have relaxed (1).	3 3

I would award this answer .... out of 6 marks because ....

Improve the answer

1 Write an improved answer to the question below. Use the hint to make sure your answer achieves the highest possible mark.

3.1 Stretching is usually carried out before and after participation in exercise.

Explain why a person should take part in stretching exercises after doing sport and physical activity. **(3)**

Had a go

It helps the muscles to recover from exercise.

> **Hint**
> This student's answer does not go far enough in its explanation. What does the stretching process do and why is this important?

....
....
....
....

---

2 Write an improved answer to the question below. Use the hints to make sure your answer achieves the highest possible mark.

3.2 Explain why a long-distance runner may be tempted to take erythropoietin (EPO) to improve their performance. **(4)**

Had a go

EPO is used to increase the number of red blood cells. This means more oxygen can be carried around the body, so will help the runner travel for a longer distance.

> **Hints**
> - This answer identifies the function of EPO. However, there is no explanation as to why having more red blood cells means more oxygen can be carried around the body. A link needs to be made to red blood cells containing haemoglobin, which transports oxygen.
> - There is no explanation of why having more oxygen will be beneficial in long-distance running. To gain credit for application to long-distance running performance, a link needs to be made to the aerobic energy system using oxygen to provide energy or ATP (adenosine triphosphate).

....
....
....
....
....
....

> I always underline the command word in a question, in this case 'Explain'. It helps me focus my answer on what the question is asking, rather than what I want it to ask.

Find the answer

1 Use the mark scheme to find the **two** answers that would be awarded 2 marks. Choose two from **A**, **B** and **C**. Explain your choice.

3.3 Maximal heart rate (MHR) is used to help work out the intensity a person should exercise at to target specific components of fitness.

Calculate the MHR of a person who is 23 years old. **(2)**

> **Hint**
> Make sure you learn the equation to work out a person's MHR (220 minus the person's age), as you may not be given this equation in the exam.

Question	Answer	Extra information	Mark
3.3	220 – 23 = 197	1 mark for correct equation Up to a maximum of 2 marks for correct answer	2

> **Hint**
> Two of the answers given here would be awarded full marks.

A   220 – 23 = 203   **B**   220 – 23 = 197   **C**   197

Answers ________ and ________ would be awarded 2 marks because ....

....

....

2 Use the mark scheme to find the answer that would be awarded 2 marks. Choose **A**, **B** or **C**. Explain your choice.

3.4 State **two** types of injury that can occur when taking part in physical activity and sport. **(2)**

Question	Answer			Mark
3.4	One mark for each correct factor. Any two from: • concussion • fracture • dislocation	• strain • tennis elbow • sprain	• golfer's elbow • abrasion • torn cartilage.	2

A   Sprained ankle, sprained wrist

B   Fracture, concussion

C   Concussion, head injury

> When answering 'State' questions, I always try to keep my answers as to-the-point as possible. There's no need to explain the answer by adding extra detail or examples. Doing this would only waste valuable time that I could spend answering longer questions.

Answer ________ would be awarded 2 marks because ....

....

....

....

Mark the answer

1 Use the mark scheme below to decide how many marks you would award the student's answer. Give reasons for your decision.

4.1 Jackie takes part in 5k and 10k cross-country races. She takes part in continuous training and fartlek training.

Evaluate which method of training would be most suitable for Jackie to improve her cross-country running performance.

(9)

> **Hints**
> This question has 'Evaluate' as the command verb. This means the response should:
> - apply technical knowledge and understanding of how each training method can improve cross-country running performance
> - contain reasoned judgements evaluating which type of training would be most suitable for Jackie to improve her cross-country running performance
> - end with a conclusion that selects one training method as the most preferable to improve cross-country running performance.

Had a go

Fartlek would be good because it involves running at different speeds, which is like cross-country running. Continuous running is also good as this involves running at the same pace at a moderate intensity for at least 20 minutes, so this will train her aerobic endurance, which is needed for cross-country running.

In conclusion, both types of training would be good for Jackie.

Level	Mark	Descriptor
	0	
1	1–3	• Demonstrates isolated elements of knowledge and understanding, with limited technical language used. • Limited attempt to apply knowledge to question context. • Generic assertions may be presented.
2	4–6	• Demonstrates mostly accurate knowledge and understanding, including appropriate use of technical language in places. • Applies knowledge to question context. • Attempts at drawing conclusion, with some support from relevant evidence.
3	7–9	• Demonstrates accurate knowledge and understanding throughout, including appropriate use of technical language. • Applies detailed knowledge to question context throughout. • Reaches valid and well-reasoned conclusions supported by relevant evidence.

I would award this answer   out of 9 marks because

Reorder the answer

1 Rearrange the sentences into the most logical order by numbering each part of the student's answer.

> **4.2** Describe the process of the passage of blood from the body to the heart and then from the heart to the lungs. **(4)**
>
> **Hint**
> It is important that answers to this type of question are in a logical order. Make sure you read your answer through from the start to check it makes sense.
>
> ☐ Blood returns to the heart through the pulmonary vein.
>
> ☐ Blood travels from the body to the heart through the vena cava.
>
> ☐ Blood travels through the pulmonary artery to the lungs.
>
> ☐ Blood travels to the body through the aorta.

2 Rearrange the sentences into the most logical order by numbering each part of the student's answer.

> **4.3** Explain the process of gaseous exchange in the lungs. **(4)**
>
> Then I would just need to check the order of the sentences to ensure they are in the correct sequence.
>
> ☐ There is a higher concentration of carbon dioxide in the blood than in the lungs.
>
> ☐ Oxygen diffuses from the alveoli into the blood.
>
> ☐ There is a higher concentration of oxygen in the lungs than in the blood.
>
> ☐ Carbon dioxide diffuses out of the blood into the alveoli.

Complete the question

1 Complete the question by adding **two** multiple-choice options. Make sure one is correct.

5.1 Which **one** of the following is the correct word equation for aerobic respiration? **(1)**

- ☐ **A** glucose + oxygen ➔ carbon dioxide + energy
- ☐ **B** glucose ➔ carbon dioxide
- ☐ **C** ....
- ☑ **D** ....

To support my revision, I created a set of key word revision cards. These were especially useful to help learn key terms that might come up in the exam.

2 Use the answer below to complete the question.

5.2 **Figure 2** shows the cardiac output of a person taking part in physical activity.

Identify the **two** factors that .... **(1)**

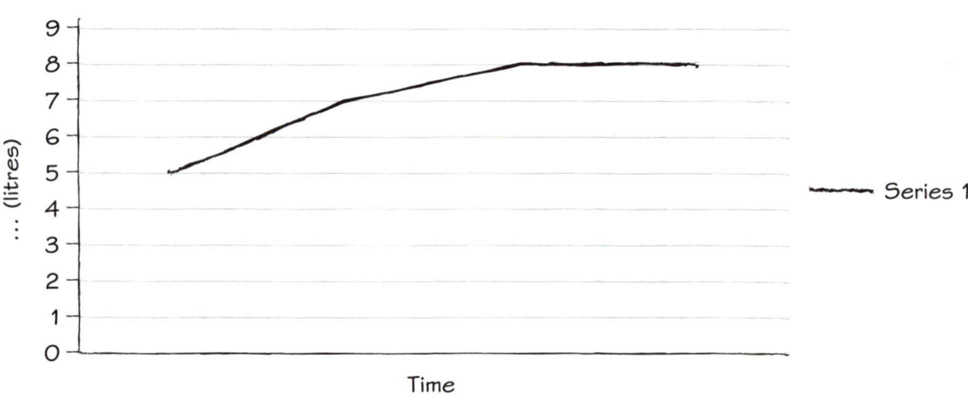

Figure 2

- ☐ **A** Tidal volume and heart rate
- ☑ **B** Stroke volume and heart rate
- ☐ **C** Blood pressure and stroke volume
- ☐ **D** Stroke volume and tidal volume

Complete the answer

1 Complete the student's answer so that it would be awarded 3 marks.

5.3 Jessie takes part in long-distance running.

Explain why red blood cells are important to athletes who take part in long-distance running events. **(3)**

> **Hint**
> If a question asks you to 'Explain', you need to make a clear point and then give further information or an example to reinforce that point. Your answer must contain some linked reasoning, so use connectives such as 'because', 'therefore', 'as a result' and 'this means that' to show your links.

Nearly there

Red blood cells contain haemoglobin, which transports oxygen around the body. Oxygen is

necessary for long-distance running because

....

2 Complete the student's answer so that it would be awarded 2 marks.

5.4 Devi takes part in football.

Giving an example, state **one** method Devi could use to reduce the risk of injury during a football match. **(2)**

> **Hint**
> This question asks you to state an example of something that Devi could do to reduce the risk of injury (such as wear protective equipment) to gain the first mark, and then state how it reduces the risk of injury to gain the second mark.

Nearly there

Devi could wear .... because these help protect

the lower leg from being kicked and getting bruised in a game of football.

3 Complete the student's answer so that it would be awarded 3 marks.

5.5 Explain how blood flow increases to the working muscles when someone is taking part in sport and physical activity. **(3)**

Nearly there

Blood vessels vasodilate. This means that

....

As a result, more blood is

> I always try to leave time at the end of an exam to go back and check what I have written. Sometimes I find a silly mistake or realise I need to add another sentence to develop my explanation.

Reorder the answer

1 Rearrange the sentences into the most logical order by numbering each part of the student's answer.

6.1 Explain why a javelin thrower may be tempted to take anabolic steroids to illegally improve their performance. **(4)**

☐ Power is a product of strength and speed.

☐ This helps to increase muscle strength.

☐ Anabolic steroids help to increase the growth of muscle tissue.

☐ This would be beneficial for a javelin thrower as they need high levels of power in their sport.

> Once I have decided which order the statements should be in, I always read them through in that order to double check that they make sense.

2 Rearrange the sentences into the most logical order by numbering each part of the student's answer.

6.2 Ellie is 28 years old. She takes part in a six-week training programme that involves running to increase her cardiovascular endurance.

Table 4 shows Ellie's resting heart rate over the six-week period.

	Week 1	Week 2	Week 3	Week 4	Week 5	Week 6
Resting heart rate (bpm)	78	72	73	72	71	70

Table 4

Using the data in **Table 4**, analyse why Ellie's resting heart rate has changed over the course of the six-week training programme. **(4)**

Hint
When analysing data, your first point should always state what the data are showing.

☐ This means the heart is able to pump out more blood per beat.

☐ This is because cardiovascular training has resulted in cardiac hypertrophy.

☐ Her resting heart rate has decreased.

☐ Yet the heart can still produce the same cardiac output.

Find the answer

1 Use the mark scheme to find the answer that would be awarded 2 marks. Choose **A**, **B**, **C** or **D**. Explain your choice.

6.3 **Figure 3** shows a gymnast performing a cartwheel.

Analyse the plane and axis of movement that this movement takes part in. **(2)**

Figure 3

Question	Answer	Mark
6.3	1 mark each for: • the plane of movement is the frontal plane (1) • the axis of movement is the sagittal (1).	2

> **Hint**
> These student answers need to cover both points in the mark scheme to gain the full 2 marks. In this case, this means including the key words 'frontal plane' and 'sagittal axis'.

A The cartwheel is performed through the frontal axis and transverse plane.

B The person is travelling through the frontal plane and rotating around the vertical axis.

C The movement takes place in the frontal plane and the rotation occurs around the sagittal axis.

D The cartwheel movement is complicated and uses both the frontal axis and sagittal plane.

> **Hint**
> Remember: the axis is the rotation point, so think about where the body is rotating when performing a cartwheel.

Answer .... would be awarded 2 marks because ....

....

....

Mark the answer

1 Draw lines to connect each of the marker's comments to the relevant part of the student's answer.

7.1 Fitness tests are used to assess specific components of fitness and to determine whether training methods should be used to develop those specific components.

Complete **Table 5** by:

(a) stating a fitness test that can be used to test each component of fitness **(3)**

(b) giving an example of a training method that can be used to develop each component of fitness. **(3)**

> Incorrect. This test measures agility, not cardiovascular fitness.

> The student has correctly identified a training method that improves cardiovascular fitness.

Component of fitness	(a) Fitness test	(b) Training method
Cardiovascular fitness	Illinois agility test .... (1)	Continuous training .... (1)
Speed	30 m sprint test .... (1)	Interval training .... (1)
Power	Grip dynamometer .... (1)	Circuit training .... (1)

> The student has chosen a suitable training method to improve speed.

Table 5

> This fitness test measures strength, not power.

> The student has correctly identified an appropriate fitness test for speed.

> Circuit training is not an appropriate training method for this component of fitness. The correct answer is plyometrics.

2 Now use the mark scheme below to decide how many marks you would award the student's answer. Give reasons for your mark.

Question	Answer			Mark
	(a) 1 mark for each correct response for each component of fitness. (b) 1 mark for each correct response for each component of fitness.			
7.1	**Component of fitness**	**(a) Fitness test**	**(b) Training method**	3 3
	Cardiovascular fitness	Cooper 12-minute test (1) Harvard step test (1)	Continuous training (1) Fartlek (1)	
	Speed	30 m sprint test (1)	Interval training (1)	
	Power	Vertical jump test (1)	Plyometrics (1)	

I would award the student's answer .... out of 6 marks because ....

....

....

....

....

Complete the question

1 Complete the question by adding **two** multiple-choice options. Make sure one is correct.

7.2 Which **one** of the following types of bones is most suitable for protecting internal organs? **(1)**

> **Hint**
> Remember: some bones of the skeleton protect internal organs. For example, the cranium protects the brain and the sternum protects the heart and lungs.

☐ **A** Long

☐ **B** Irregular

☑ **C** ....

☐ **D** ....

2 Complete the question by adding **two** multiple-choice options. Make sure one is correct.

7.3 Which **one** of the following is a waste product from anaerobic respiration? **(1)**

> **Hint**
> Multiple-choice options are always believable answers. Imagine you are trying to trip up another student with your incorrect option.

☑ **A** ....

☐ **B** ....

☐ **C** Glucose

☐ **D** Oxygen

3 Complete the question by adding the correct multiple-choice option.

7.4 Which **one** of the following is the classification of joint found at the hip? **(1)**

☐ **A** Pivot

☑ **B** ....

☐ **C** Hinge

☐ **D** Condyloid

Mark the answer

1 Use the mark scheme below to decide how many marks you would award the student's answer. Give reasons for your mark.

7.5 Skeletal muscle is made up of three different fibre types.

Assess the importance of the following fibre types for a long-distance road cyclist:

(a) Type I **(3)**

Had a go

Type I muscle fibres produce low force so are used to keep going for the whole race.

> **Hint**
> The student would gain credit for knowledge relating to 'keep going for the whole race' as this links to the fact that these muscle fiibre types are slow to fatigue. Further credit would be given for 'produce low force' as this is another characteristic of Type I muscle fibres. To gain more credit, this could have been linked to when the cyclist is on a flat part of the race and therefore needing only a low force to push the pedals.

(b) Type IIx **(3)**

Had a go

Type IIx muscle fibres produce high force so are not used much in the race.

Question	Answer	Mark
7.5 (a)	1 mark for each of the following linked points. • Type I fibres produce low force (1) and are resistant to fatigue (1) as they need to contract for long periods during a long-distance race (1).	3
7.5 (b)	1 mark for each of the following points. • Type IIx fibres produce high force (1) and contract quickly (1) so would be used for a sprint finish at the end of the cycle race (1).	3

I would award the student's answer .... out of 6 marks because ....

....

....

....

....

....

....

....

....

....

When revising, I find it really helpful to look at good and poor answers to exam questions. This helps me understand what the examiner is looking for.

Complete the answer

1 Complete the student's answer so that it would be awarded 4 marks.

8.1 Jenny takes part in cross-country running. During one run she sprains her ankle.

Explain how Jenny should use the process of RICE to treat her sprained ankle. **(4)**

> **Hint**
> The question asks how RICE should be carried out, so you don't need to write about each part of the process in detail. Just state what needs to be done to treat the injury.

Had a go

RICE should be used as it does the following:

R – this means .... and it means Jenny should

I – this means .... so Jenny should

C – this stands for .... and to do this Jenny should put a bandage around her ankle.

E – this means .... so Jenny should

2 Complete the student's answer so that it would be awarded 4 marks.

8.2 Explain how the muscles in an antagonistic muscle pair work together to produce movement. **(4)**

> **Hint**
> Remember: muscles are only able to contract and relax. In an antagonistic muscle pair, to produce movement one muscle contracts while the other muscle relaxes.

> **Hint**
> This question is worth 4 marks, so only a simple explanation is required. For any antagonistic muscle pair, make sure you use the correct terminology to refer to the muscle that contracts and the muscle that relaxes.

Had a go

An antagonistic muscle pair is where one muscle in the pair contracts to produce movement.

This muscle is called the

The other muscle in the pair is the antagonist. This muscle

> After I have completed my answer to a question, I always read it back to myself to make sure it makes sense and to check that I have used the correct PE terminology.

Complete the question

1 Use the hints and the student's answers below to complete questions 8.3 (a) and 8.3 (b).

8.3 **Figure 4** shows a person's heart rate at rest and during exercise.

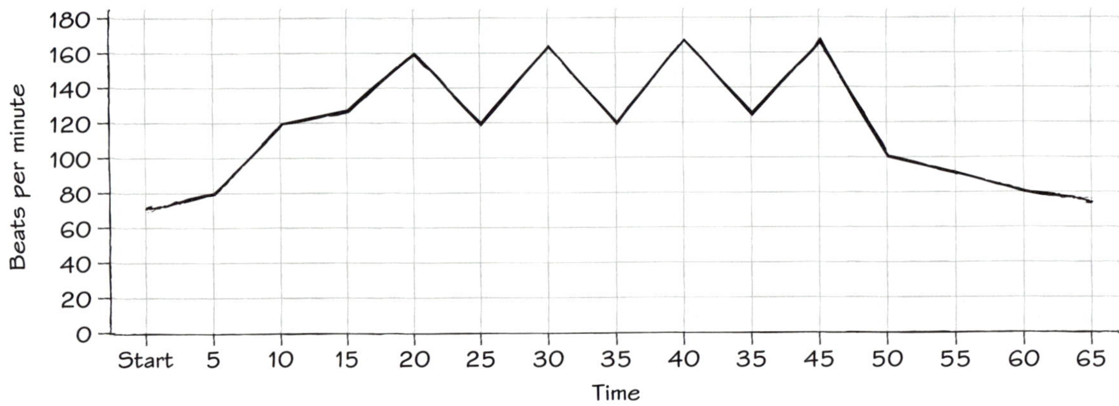

Figure 4

(a) Using the graph, explain why the person's ....

.... **(3)**

> **Hint**
> Notice how **Figure 4** shows the person's heart rate increase from just over 70 beats per minute to 80 beats per minute while at rest. The student's answer explains why this has occurred. What question could you ask to prompt this response?

Nailed it!

The heart rate has increased because of the anticipatory increase in heart rate, where a person increases their heart rate simply by thinking about exercise. This increase in heart rate has the effect of preparing the body for exercise.

(b) Using the graph, explain ....

.... **(3)**

> **Hint**
> Read through the student's answer carefully and consider what it is explaining. Do any of the sentences in the student's answer appear to answer the question directly? If they do, this will give you a big clue as to the original question.

Nailed it!

The person could be taking part in interval training. This is because there are periods of high-intensity exercise where the heart rate is high and then rest periods where the heart rate decreases as they are working at a lower intensity.

> I find it useful to create my own examples of questions as part of my revision. It really helps me understand what the examiner is looking for.

Find the answer

1 Use the mark scheme to find the student answer that would be awarded full marks. Choose **A**, **B**, **C** or **D**.

8.4 **Figure 5** shows a lever system.

Identify the parts of the lever system. (3)

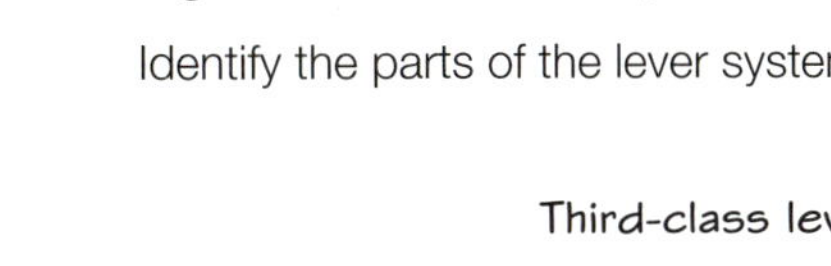

Figure 5

> **Hint**
> Remember: a lever system consists of three main parts. You need to be able to name each part and describe what it does. In **Figure 5**, each part is represented by an arrow pointing in the direction of the force.

Question	Answer	Mark
8.4	One mark for each part of diagram correctly identified: A – fulcrum (1) B – effort (1) C – load (1).	3

A   Part A is the effort, part B is the load and part C is the fulcrum.

B   Part A is the fulcrum, part B is the load and part C is the effort.

C   Part A is the fulcrum, part B is the effort and part C is the load.

D   Part A is the load, part B is the effort and part C is the fulcrum

Answer .... would be awarded 3 marks because ....

....

....

....

....

....

Find the answer

1 Use the mark scheme to find the student answer that would be awarded full marks. Choose **A**, **B**, **C** or **D**.

9.1 Describe a third-class lever system found in the body. (4)

> **Hint**
> Remember: the location of each part of the lever system determines which type of lever it is.

I always use the mnemonic 'FLE' to help me remember which lever system is which.
- First-class lever systems have the **F**ulcrum in the middle.
- Second-class lever systems have the **L**oad in the middle.
- Third-class lever systems have the **E**ffort in the middle.

Question	Answer	Mark
9.1	Award marks for: • location in body (1) • identification of effort in body (1) • identification of fulcrum in body (1) • identification of load in body (1). For example: • At the arm (1), with the biceps producing effort (1), the elbow acting as the fulcrum (1), and the hand and lower arm acting as the load (1).	4

A This type of lever can be found in the arm, with the elbow as the fulcrum and the weight of the hand as the load.

B The arm has this type of lever, with the biceps producing the effort, the elbow acting as the fulcrum, and the lower arm and hand (and anything the hand is holding) acting as the load.

C The arm is a third-class lever. The elbow acts as the fulcrum, the triceps produce the effort, and the hand is the load.

D A third-class lever can be found in the arm, with the fulcrum at the elbow.

Answer .... would be awarded 4 marks because ....

....

....

....

I really struggled with understanding where the three types of lever system are found in the body, so I learned specific examples of each type and the bones, muscles and joints involved. I even practised moving my body while calling out the different names and their role in the lever system – this made the theory so much easier to understand!

Mark the answer

1 Use the mark scheme below to decide how many marks you would award the student's answer. Give reasons for your mark.

9.2 **Figure 6** is a diagram of the skeletal system.

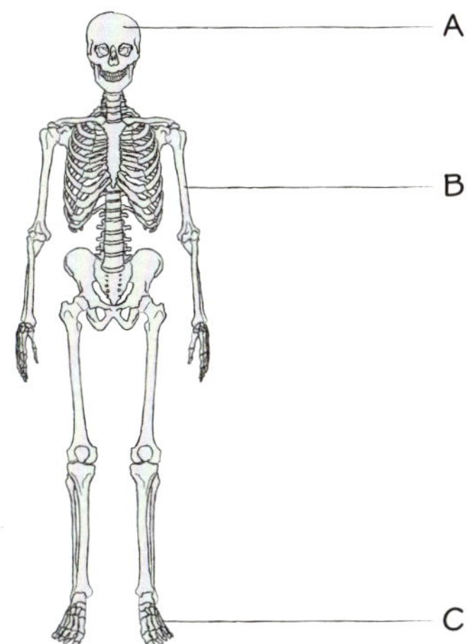

Figure 6

Complete **Table 6** by:

(a) identifying the bones labelled A, B and C (3)

(b) for each bone identified, stating the type of bone. (3)

> **Hint**
> You need to learn the names of the following bones and their location in the body: cranium, clavicle, scapula, the five regions of the vertebral column (cervical, thoracic, lumbar, sacrum, coccyx), ribs, sternum, humerus, radius, ulna, carpals, metacarpals, phalanges (in the hand), pelvis, femur, patella, tibia, fibula, tarsals, metatarsals and phalanges in the foot.

	(a) Name of bone	(b) Type of bone
A	Cranium	Irregular
B	Humerus	Long
C	Carpals	Sesamoid

Table 6

Question	Answer				Mark
9.2	One mark for each correct answer.				6
			(a) Name of bone	(b) Type of bone	
		A	Cranium (1)	Flat (1)	
		B	Humerus (1)	Long (1)	
		C	Metatarsals (1)	Short (1)	

I would give the student's answer .... out of 6 marks because ....

....

....

....

....

Mark the answer

1 Use the mark scheme to find the student answer that would be awarded full marks. Choose **A**, **B**, **C** or **D**. Explain your choice.

9.3 An athlete has a resting heart rate of 56 beats per minute and a resting stroke volume of 1000 ml.

Calculate the resting cardiac output for this athlete. (2)

> **Hint**
> You need to know the equation for cardiac output for this question. Remember: $Q = SV \times HR$

Question	Answer	Mark
9.3	1 mark for correct equation; 1 mark for correct calculation. • $Q = SV \times HR$ or $Q = HR \times SV$ (1) • $Q = 56 \times 1000 = 56{,}000$ ml per minute / 56 l per minute (1)	2

A   56 l per minute

B $Q = SV \times HR = 5600$ ml per minute

C $Q = HR \times SV = 56$ l per minute

D $Q = HR \times SV = 56{,}000$ ml per hour

Answer .... would be awarded full marks because ....

....

....

....

2 Now use the mark scheme above to find the student answers that would **not** be awarded full marks. Choose **A**, **B**, **C** or **D**. Explain your choice.

Answer .... would not be awarded full marks because, ...

....

....

Answer .... would not be awarded full marks because, ...

....

....

Answer .... would not be awarded full marks because, ...

....

....

Complete the answer

1 Use the hints below to complete the student's answers so that parts (a) and (b) would each be awarded 3 marks.

10.1 Vasilis takes part in a cycle race. The race involves cycling 75 miles, mainly on flat roads but with some steep hills.

(a) Explain the type of muscle fibres used by Vasilis on flat roads during the cycle race. **(3)**

> **Hint**
> The race is a long distance one, so it is important that the muscle fibres do not fatigue. You need to complete the student's answer by explaining why Type I muscle fibres would mostly be used during the flat parts of the race.

Had a go

Vasilis would use type I muscle fibres on the flat roads because ....

....

....

(b) Explain the type of muscle fibres used by Vasilis to climb steep hills during the cycle race. **(3)**

> **Hint**
> There are two types of fast-twitch muscle fibre. The type that produces the highest force would be most appropriate for cycling up a hill. You need to complete the student's answer by explaining why.

Had a go

Vasilis would use type IIx muscle fibres for cycling up hills because ....

....

....

---

2 Complete the student's answer so that it would be awarded 4 marks.

10.2 Explain **two** characteristics of type IIx muscle fibres. **(4)**

Nearly there

Characteristic 1: Type IIx muscle fibres fatigue quickly as they ....

....

Nearly there

Characteristic 2: Type IIx muscle fibres can contract quickly, which means ....

....

> I find it really helpful to underline the key words in a question, especially when the question is long. It helps me focus on what I have to do.

Reorder the answer

1 Rearrange the sentences into the most logical order by numbering each part of the student's answer.

10.3 Explain the process of gaseous exchange in the lungs. **(4)**

> **Hint**
> Remember: the process of gaseous exchange starts with taking air into the lungs. Gaseous exchange gets oxygen into the bloodstream and removes carbon dioxide from the body.

☐ Carbon dioxide diffuses from a high concentration in the blood to a low concentration in the alveoli.

☐ Oxygen diffuses from a high concentration in the alveoli to a low concentration in the bloodstream.

☐ Air is breathed into the lungs.

☐ The carbon dioxide is then breathed out.

---

2 Rearrange the sentences into the most logical order by numbering each part of the student's answer.

10.4 Explain the process of blood flow through the heart to the lungs and body. **(4)**

> **Hint**
> It is important that answers to this type of question are in a logical order. Make sure you read your answer through from the start to check it makes sense.

☐ Blood then flows to the right ventricle, which contracts to push blood to the lungs.

☐ Blood then flows to the left ventricle, which contracts to push blood to the body.

☐ Blood flows from the lungs to the left atrium.

☐ Blood flows from the body into the right atrium.

Improve the answer

1 Use the hint below to write an improved student answer that would be awarded 2 marks.

10.5 Blood is made up of red and white blood cells, platelets and plasma.

(a) Describe the function of red blood cells. (2)

Had a go

The function of red blood cells is to carry oxygen around the body.

Hint

To gain the full 2 marks for a 'Describe' question, you need to identify what has been asked for (the 'function of red blood cells') then describe how this is done by giving further details. This student's answer would only gain the first mark. Improve the answer so it would be awarded full marks.

2 Use the hint below to write an improved student answer that would be awarded 2 marks.

(b) Describe the function of white blood cells. (2)

Had a go

White blood cells fight infection.

Hint

As the question is worth 2 marks, you will need to make two distinct points to be awarded full marks. This student's answer only makes one distinct point. To improve the answer, you need to go on to describe how white blood cells do this.

I always underline the command word in a question ('Describe', in this instance). It helps me focus my answer on what the question is asking rather than what I want it to ask.

Mark the answer

1 Draw lines to connect each of the marker's comments to the relevant part of the student's answer.

11.1 **Figure 7** shows a batsman hitting a ball in cricket.

Explain, giving an example for each, **two** different methods used to reduce the risk of a batsman getting injured during a cricket match.

(4)

Figure 7

Hint

To achieve full marks for this question, you need to identify **two** different methods of injury prevention for a batsman and then explain how each method works to prevent injury.

Had a go

He could wear a helmet on his head to help

to reduce the risk of getting injured when

batting in cricket.

He could also wear gloves to keep his hands

warm and help him grip the bat so he can hit

the ball with more force.

An example of what the cricketer is wearing has been provided.

The reason provided does not reduce the risk of injury, so no marks would be awarded for this point.

The student has chosen an appropriate method of protection for the batsman's head.

The student has not given any form of injury that could occur to the head, so no marks would be awarded for this part of the response.

2 Now use the mark scheme below to help you decide how many marks you would award the student's answer above. Give reasons for your mark.

Question	Answer	Mark
11.1	One mark for each appropriate method identified and one mark for each linked explanation. For example: • He could wear a helmet (1) as this will help to protect his head from being hit by the ball when it is bowled at him and help prevent him getting concussion (1). • He could wear gloves (1) as these will help to protect his hands from being hit by the ball when it is bowled at him and help prevent him fracturing a bone (1).	4

I would award the student's answer ...... marks because

Find the answer

1 Use the mark scheme to find the student's answer that would be awarded 3 marks. Choose **A**, **B**, **C** or **D**. Explain your choice.

11.2 When a person is taking part in exercise, blood is redirected to the working muscles.

Explain how blood is redirected to the working muscles. (3)

Question	Answer	Mark
11.2	1 mark for identification, 1 further mark for each explanatory point. • The blood vessels vasodilate (1), which means the lumen widens (1) to allow more blood to flow though the arterioles leading to the working muscles (1).	3

A More blood goes to the working muscles because the blood vessels leading to the muscles increase in size. This is called vasoconstriction.

B The lumen of the blood vessels increase in size, which is called vasodilation. This increases the size of the lumen of the arterioles leading to the working muscles, so more blood flows to the working muscles.

C The size of the lumen of the arterioles increases, which means more blood can flow through them as they dilate, allowing more blood flow to the working muscles.

> **Hint**
> The technical term vasodilation must be used, as this literally means 'blood vessel increasing in size'. The opposite is vasoconstriction. Make sure you don't get the two terms confused!

Answer .... would be awarded 3 marks because ....

....

....

....

Reorder the answer

1 Rearrange the sentences into the most logical order by numbering each part of the student's answer.

11.3 Describe the process of carrying out a sit-and-reach test. (4)

> **Hint**
> It is important that answers to this type of question are in a logical order. Make sure you read your final answer through from the start, to check it makes sense.

☐ They hold the stretch for one to two seconds while the reading is recorded.

☐ They sit on the floor with their legs out straight in front of them and lean forward, keeping their knees on the ground.

☐ They position their hands with the palms facing down on the measuring box and move their hands along the measuring line as far as possible.

☐ The person carries out a warm up.

2 Rearrange the sentences into the most logical order by numbering each part of the student's answer.

11.4 Describe the process of carrying out a Cooper 12-minute run test. (4)

☐ The distance the person covered in 12 minutes is measured and recorded.

☐ The person carries out a warm up.

☐ The stopwatch is started. The person starts to run.

☐ When 12 minutes have passed the person is told to stop running.

To support my revision, I created revision cards that numbered the different stages of each fitness test. These were really useful to help me revise the differences between each test.

Complete the answer

1 Use the hint below to complete the student's answer so that it would be awarded 6 marks.

12.1 Explain **two** functions of the respiratory system that enable a long-distance swimmer to perform well in their event.

(6)

> **Hint**
> To achieve full marks, for each function of the respiratory system your answer needs to:
> * link the function to swimming performance
> * justify how it enables the swimmer to perform well.

Function 1:

Had a go

The respiratory system allows oxygen to be taken in so that ....

....

....

Function 2:

Had a go

The respiratory system removes carbon dioxide, which is ....

....

....

2 Use the hint below to complete the student's answer so that it would be awarded 6 marks.

12.2 Explain **two** functions of the cardiovascular system that enable a cross-country runner to perform well in their event.

(6)

> **Hint**
> To achieve full marks, for each function of the cardiovascular system your answer needs to:
> * link the function to cross-country running performance
> * justify how it enables the cross-country runner to perform well.

Function 1:

Had a go

The cardiovascular system carries glucose in the blood. ....

....

....

Function 2:

Had a go

The cardiovascular system removes carbon dioxide, which is ....

....

....

Improve the answer

1 Use the hints to write an improved student answer that could be awarded 9 marks.

12.3 Hans is an athlete who takes part in the high jump. His training programme includes plyometrics, circuit training and sprint interval training.

Evaluate the likely effects of these training methods on Hans's fitness for his high-jump performance. **(9)**

Had a go

Plyometric training is used to train power. Power is needed in the high jump to be able to do well. If Hans did not have high levels of power, he would not be able to perform well in his sport.

Circuit training improves stamina, which is not needed in the high jump.

Sprint interval training will increase speed. Speed is used in the run-up of the high jump, as this helps the high jumper to jump higher.

Hints

- The student has correctly identified the component of fitness that is developed using plyometrics. They now need to explain what power is used for in the high jump and give a judgement about the value of this training method in improving high-jump performance.
- Stamina is not a component of fitness and this term will not get any credit. Make sure you use the correct terminology for components of fitness. In this example, circuits will develop cardiovascular fitness.
- The student has correctly identified sprinting as the component of fitness developed by interval training. However, the reason given for how speed helps with high-jump performance is not credit-worthy: the student needs to explain how it increases momentum, which increases the height that can be jumped.

Complete the question

1 Complete the question by adding **two** multiple-choice options. Make sure only one is correct.

12.4 Which **one** of the following percentage ranges of maximal heart rate is the aerobic training zone? **(1)**

☐ **A** 100%

☐ **B** ....

☑ **C** ....

☐ **D** 50–60%

> **Hint**
> Multiple-choice answers always contain believable answers. Make sure your incorrect option really tests a student's understanding of the aerobic training zone.

2 Complete the question by adding **three** multiple-choice options. Make sure only one is correct.

12.5 Which **one** of the following is the chamber in the heart that receives deoxygenated blood from the body? **(1)**

☐ **A** Right ventricle

☐ **B** ....

☐ **C** ....

☑ **D** ....

> **Hint**
> Remember: there are four chambers in the heart and you will need to identify them all to complete this multiple-choice question. Make sure you put the right answer against the box with the tick!

Mark the answer

1 Draw lines to connect each of the marker's comments to the relevant part of the student's answer.

12.6 Different muscle fibre types are used for participation in different types of sport and physical activity.

Explain which muscle fibre type would mainly be used in 100 m sprinting events. **(3)**

> **Hint**
> Remember: there are three muscle fibre types: type I, type IIa and type IIx.

Nailed it!

The muscle fibre type that would mainly be used is type IIx. This type of muscle fibre is able to contract very quickly. It is used in the 100 m sprint as the competitor needs to move very fast.

The student has identified the correct muscle fibre type.

The student has correctly identified a characteristic of this muscle fibre type.

The student has successfully linked their answer to sprinting performance.

12.7 Different muscle fibre types are used for participation in different types of sport and physical activity.

Explain which muscle fibre type would mainly be used in a 100 km cycling event. **(3)**

Nailed it!

The muscle fibre type that would mainly be used is type I. This type of muscle fibre is able to contract for long periods of time without fatiguing. It is used in the 100 km cycle race as the cyclist needs to continually pedal, which requires sustained muscular contractions.

The student has identified the correct muscle fibre type.

The student has correctly identified a characteristic of this muscle fibre type.

The student has successfully linked their answer to long-distance cycling performance.

I always make sure I read the question carefully and check what I am being asked. I've learned from past mistakes that I can get carried away and not realise until I've wasted precious time that I've answered the wrong question!

Complete the answer

1 Use the hint below to complete the student's answer so that it would be awarded 3 marks.

13.1 Explain why it is important that a rest day is included in a weekly training programme in order for fitness levels to increase. (3)

> **Hint**
> Think about what happens during the recovery process and why this is important for a person to be able to improve their fitness levels.

Had a go

A rest day helps the body to recover.

2 Use the hint below to rewrite the student's answer so that it would be awarded 3 marks.

13.2 Explain why progressive overload is important in a training programme. (3)

> **Hint**
> The student begins their response by giving a definition of what progressive overload is. You need to complete the answer by providing explanatory points about why progressive overload is important in a training programme. Think about how it helps the body to improve and what it protects it from.

Had a go

Progressive overload is the process of gradually increasing how hard a person works when training. It is important so that a person's body

Improve the answer

1 Use the hint below to write an improved student answer that would be awarded 3 marks.

13.3 Movement in physical activities and sport occurs in different planes.

Figure 8 shows a gymnast performing a star jump.

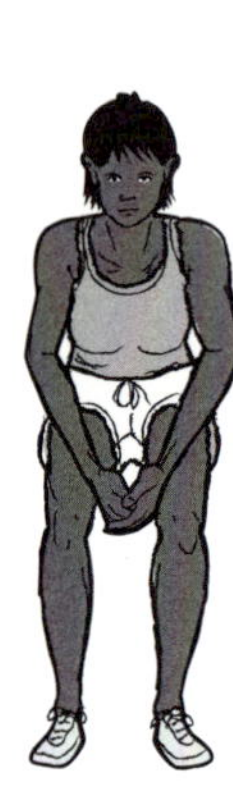

Figure 8

Analyse the plane and axis of movement involved in a star jump.

(3)

Had a go

The movement is a star jump, and the hips and shoulders produce movement.

The movement is taking place in the frontal plane.

> **Hint**
> Think about the types of movement that take place when performing a star jump.
> Look at the hips and shoulders – what type of movement occurs at these joints? This will help you to work out which plane of movement is involved. From this, you can determine the axis of movement.

When answering exam questions, I always follow this fail-safe method: I read the question, then look at the number of marks available, then read the question again and decide how many points I need to make for each part of the question. This approach really helped me get my timings right in the exam.

Complete the question

1 Use the hint below to write an improved student answer that would be awarded 3 marks.

13.4 Figure 9 shows a person **preparing** to kick a rugby ball.

Figure 9

Complete **Table 7** by:

(a) identifying the type of movement at the knee

(b) identifying the plane of movement at the knee

(c) identifying the axis of movement at the knee   (3)

Had a go

Joint	Knee
(a) Type of movement	Bend the knee
(b) Plane of movement	Frontal
(c) Axis of movement	Frontal

Table 7

> **Hint**
> 'Bend' is not a technical term, so no credit would be awarded here. Remember: the plane
> and axis of movement will always be different – there is no movement that has the same plane
> and axis.

Joint	Knee
(a) Type of movement	
(b) Plane of movement	
(c) Axis of movement	

Table 7

Find the answer

1 Use the mark scheme to find the answer that would be awarded 4 marks. Choose **A**, **B** or **C**.

13.5 Analyse the role of red blood cells for long-distance cycling. **(4)**

Question	Answer	Mark
13.5	(1) mark for each point up to 4 marks. Red blood cells carry oxygen (1) as they contain haemoglobin, which binds oxygen (1). Oxygen is needed by the aerobic energy system (1), which is the main method of supplying ATP during long-distance cycling (1).	4

Hint

Remember to check each answer against the mark scheme closely to make sure it covers all four points, otherwise the answer can't be awarded the full 4 marks.

A Oxygen is transported in the red blood cells because they have haemoglobin. A long-distance cyclist will supply ATP using the aerobic energy system, so they need high levels of oxygen.

B Red blood cells contain haemoglobin. Oxygen is carried by haemoglobin, so the more red blood cells there are in the blood the more oxygen can be carried. Oxygen is used for the aerobic energy system. A long-distance cyclist needs lots of energy.

C The aerobic energy system supplies most of a long-distance cyclist's ATP. The aerobic energy system requires high levels of oxygen. Red blood cells carry oxygen because they contain haemoglobin, which binds oxygen to it. So having high levels of red blood cells means there is a lot of oxygen for ATP production by the aerobic energy system.

Hint

Make sure the link to sporting performance is clearly related to the function of red blood cells. You would not gain any marks for simply saying 'they provide oxygen' or 'they produce energy': you need to explain what the red blood cell provides and how this benefits cycling performance.

Answer .... would be awarded full marks because ....

....

....

....

....

....

....

....

Complete the answer

1 Complete the student's answer so that it would be awarded 3 marks.

13.6 Explain why a person should take part in an active cool down after completing sport and physical activity. **(3)**

Had a go

A cool down is necessary to help reduce muscle soreness after taking part in exercise.

....

....

....

....

....

> **Hint**
> This student's answer only gives one reason why a cool down is useful to the body.
> The student also needs to:
> - explain what a cool down does to heart rate
> - explain how taking part in a cool down can help to remove the waste product that causes muscle soreness.

2 Complete the student's answer so that it would be awarded 4 marks.

13.7 Explain why a shot-put thrower may be tempted to take anabolic steroids to improve their performance. **(4)**

> **Hint**
> The student starts their answer by stating what anabolic steroids do to muscle tissues and how this would impact on muscle strength. To complete the student's answer, you need to apply this physiological benefit to how taking anabolic steroids would improve shot-put throwing performance.

Had a go

Anabolic steroids increase the rate at which muscle tissue grows, helping to increase muscle

strength. A shot-put thrower may take anabolic steroids to

....

....

....

....

....

....

Complete the question

1 Complete the question by adding **two** multiple-choice options. Make sure one is correct.

1.1 Which **one** of the following is a micronutrient? (1)

> **Hint**
> Multiple-choice answers always contain believable answers. Make sure your incorrect option really tests students' understanding of micronutrients. You could try to catch them out by giving a type of macronutrient instead.

- [ ] **A** Fat
- [✓] **B** ....
- [ ] **C** Carbohydrate
- [ ] **D** ....

2 Complete the question by adding **two** multiple-choice options. Make sure one is correct.

1.2 Which **one** of the following is the best example of fixed practice? (1)

> **Hint**
> Remember: there are different types of practice, so you will need to know what each type involves and when it is best used.

- [ ] **A** Repeatedly practising a skill for a set period with no break for recovery
- [✓] **B** ....
- [ ] **C** ....
- [ ] **D** Repeatedly practising a skill for a set time with recovery periods

I find doing lots of different activities helps keep my revision interesting. For example, answering questions, improving existing answers, marking answers and revising my notes all helped me feel more confident.

Complete the question

1 Use the hint and the student's answers below to complete the questions.

Hint
Use the correct answers to work out what type of health benefit is being asked about.
The incorrect options for each question will help you.

1.3 Which **one** of the following is an example of a .... of regular participation in physical activity? **(1)**

- [ ] **A** Decreases the risk of depression
- [✓] **B** Helps a person meet new people and make friends
- [ ] **C** Reduces the risk of obesity
- [ ] **D** Improves mood

1.4 Which **one** of the following is an example of a .... of regular participation in physical activity? **(1)**

- [ ] **A** Decreases the risk of depression
- [ ] **B** Helps a person meet new people and make friends
- [✓] **C** Reduces the risk of obesity
- [ ] **D** Improves mood

1.5 Which **one** of the following is an example of a .... of regular participation in physical activity? **(1)**

- [✓] **A** Decreases the risk of depression
- [ ] **B** Helps a person meet new people and make friends
- [ ] **C** Reduces the risk of obesity
- [ ] **D** Decreases the risk of osteoporosis

I find it useful to make a list of key terms used in PE. This helps me understand the ideas in the question and know what it's asking.

Find the answer

1 Use the mark scheme to find the student's answer that would be awarded 2 marks. Choose **A**, **B**, **C** or **D**. Explain your decision.

2.1 Give **two** characteristics of a basic skill. (2)

Question	Answer	Mark
2.1	Requires basic movement patterns (1). Requires little decision making (1).	2

Hint
Remember: use the correct terminology in your response. In the answer to this question, a key term is 'decision making' – you should know how and when to use this term.

A The skill is performed in a stable environment. It does not need much thinking about.

B The skill needs a lot of thought and has complex movement patterns.

C The skill only uses basic movement patterns. Minimum decision making is needed.

D The skill requires complex decision making. The movement pattern is simple.

Answer .... would be awarded 2 marks because ....

....

---

2 Use the mark scheme to find the student's answer that would be awarded 1 mark. Choose **A**, **B**, **C** or **D**. Explain your decision.

2.2 Identify a sports performer who may experience enhanced performance from carbohydrate loading. (1)

Question	Answer	Mark
2.2	Any athlete involved in endurance events lasting longer than 120 minutes (1).	1

Hint
Make sure you focus on key terms in the question. Here, 'carbohydrate loading' is the key term, so you will need to consider what it means and where it could benefit sporting performance.

A A gymnast

C A badminton player

B A marathon runner

D A shot-put thrower

Answer .... would be awarded 1 mark because ....

....

Improve the answer

1 Use the hint below to write an improved student answer that would be awarded 3 marks.

2.3 Consuming alcoholic drinks is a lifestyle choice.

Explain **one** way in which consuming alcoholic drinks can negatively impact on health and wellbeing. **(3)**

Had a go

Alcoholic drinks can cause damage to the body, which can negatively affect a person's health.

> **Hint**
> This answer simply states that alcoholic drinks damage the body, so would be awarded no marks. To gain the 3 marks available, the student needs to state which part of the body is affected by drinking alcoholic drinks, then go on to explain how it is affected and why this has a negative impact on a person's health and wellbeing.

2 Use the hint below to write an improved student answer that would be awarded 2 marks.

2.4 Complete the following statements about the benefits of regular participation in physical activity.

Had a go

(a) Participation in physical activity can provide physical health benefits such as decreasing the risk of depression.

(b) An increase in the number of friends is an example of an emotional health benefit. **(2)**

> **Hint**
> Question 2.4 (a) is asking about physical health benefits. Depression is related to emotional/psychological health, so this response is incorrect. For Question 2.4 (b), emotional health is related to psychological health, which is to do with a person's state of mind. While having friends may be beneficial to a person's mental health, it relates more strongly to another type of health.

2.4 (a) Participation in physical activity can provide physical health benefits such as

....

(b) An increase in the number of friends is an example of

....

I found it useful to look at and practise as many exam questions as possible before the exam. It really helped my understanding of how to answer them successfully.

Mark the answer

1 Draw lines to connect each of the marker's comments to the relevant parts of the student's answer.

3.1 Describe **two** ways in which a sports performer can demonstrate sportsmanship. **(4)**

> **Hint**
> This question requires the student to identify two separate ways in which sportsmanship can be shown, and then describe how each way does this by giving further information or an example.

Had a go

Congratulating an opponent, which
shows that the person recognises
good sporting performance.

Time wasting, for example if a team
has the lead and wants to minimise the
opposing team's chance of getting
another goal to equalise.

This is gamesmanship, not sportsmanship.

One way has been correctly identified.

This is a good example of gamesmanship but it does not answer the question.

The student has given a good example that effectively describes how sportsmanship is demonstrated.

2 Now use the mark scheme below to decide how many marks you would award the student's answer above. Give a reason for your mark.

Question	Answer	Mark
3.1	1 mark for each identification of sportsmanship and 1 mark for each linked description. For example: • congratulating an opponent during a game (1) shows that the player recognises high levels of sporting performance (1) • calling the ball out when it rolls over the line (1) to ensure the rules are being followed fairly (1).	4

I would award the student's answer   out of 4 marks because
....
....
....
....
....
....
....

> When revising, I find looking at good and poor answers to exam questions really helps me understand what the examiner is looking for.

Reorder the answer

1 Rearrange the sentences into the most logical order by numbering each part of the student's answer.

3.2 Many club teams receive sponsorship to help to improve their players' performance in that sport.

Explain **two** ways in which sponsorship can help to improve performance in sport. **(4)**

> **Hint**
> It is important that answers to this type of question are in a logical order. Make sure you read your final answer through from the start to check it makes sense.

☐ This helps the players to develop their components of fitness, so they can perform better in the sport.

☐ Sponsorship can also pay weekly salaries to the players.

☐ This allows the players to focus on training and playing without having to spend time and energy working to earn money.

☐ Sponsorship can help to pay for new training equipment.

2 Rearrange the sentences into the most logical order by numbering each part of the student's answer.

3.3 Many club teams receive sponsorship.

Explain **two** potential negative affects of sponsorship for a club team. **(4)**

☐ This would mean fewer people are able to attend and support the team, which would demotivate the players.

☐ The sponsor may want some things done in a certain way.

☐ Seat prices for spectators may go up and become too expensive for some supporters.

☐ This may clash with the ideals of the club team.

> When answering 4-mark 'Explain' questions, I always try to think of two ideas to include in my answer **before** I start writing it.

Complete the answer

1 Complete the student's answer so that it would be awarded 3 marks.

4.1 Research has clearly linked smoking with ill health.

Explain **one** negative effect of smoking on health. **(3)**

> **Hint**
> Remember: to achieve the full 3 marks for this question, you need to list **three** things:
> - what the negative effect is (1 mark)
> - **two** points of explanation (2 marks).

Had a go

Smoking can cause .... such as bronchitis. This affects the tubes ....

entering the lungs by ....

....

....

....

....

....

....

---

2 Complete this student's answer to the same question so that it would also be awarded 3 marks.

4.1 Research has clearly linked smoking with ill health.

Explain **one** negative effect of smoking on health. **(3)**

Had a go

Smoking can cause lung .... This is where tumours ....

....

....

....

....

....

....

When answering exam questions, I always follow this fail-safe method: I read the question, then look at the number of marks available, then read the question again and decide how many points I need to make for each part of the question. This approach really helps me get my timings right in the exam.

Improve the answer

1 Use the hint below to improve the student's answer so that it would be awarded 3 marks.

4.2 Explain what is meant by coronary heart disease. (3)

Had a go

Coronary heart disease is where the blood vessels that supply blood to the heart do not work properly. This can occur because of a high-fat diet.

> **Hint**
> To achieve 3 marks for this question you need to list **three** things:
> - what coronary heart disease is – this student's answer gives a partial definition and needs to be more specific about how the blood vessels supplying the heart do not work properly
> - **two points of explanation** about how coronary heart disease occurs – this student has made one point but needs to go on to explain how a high-fat diet contributes to coronary heart disease.

....

....

....

....

2 Use the hint below to improve the student's answer so that it would be awarded 3 marks.

4.3 Explain what is meant by type 1 diabetes. (3)

Had a go

Type 1 diabetes is where blood sugar levels get too high and the person needs medicine to control it.

> **Hint**
> The student has correctly described what type 1 diabetes is. While they have stated that medicine is needed to control it, they have not specified what the medicine is. Finally, a further point needs to be made about what the medicine does/why it is needed.

....

....

....

....

> I really took the time to learn key terms used in PE, and even created flash cards to help me learn key words when revising. It meant I always knew what a question was asking me in the exam and could use the terms accurately in my answers, too.

Complete the question

1 Use the student's answer below to complete the question.

> **5.1** Define the term .... **(1)**
>
> **Nailed it!**
>
> This term means behaviour that goes against the moral values or laws of the sport.
>
> > **Hint**
> > Read the student's answer carefully. What has the student focused on in their answer? Use this information to work out what the question was asking in the first place.

2 Use the student's answer below to complete the question.

> **5.2** Explain what is meant by .... **(2)**
>
> **Nailed it!**
>
> A process by which a person increases their muscle glycogen stores by increasing the amount of carbohydrate they consume and reducing their exercise levels.

After I have completed my answer to a question, I always read it back to myself to make sure it makes sense and to check that I have used the correct PE terminology.

3 Use the student's answer below to complete the question.

> **5.3** James is learning how to take a penalty shot in football.
>
> Explain **one** way in which .... will improve James's penalty shot performance. **(3)**
>
> **Nailed it!**
>
> By seeing a demonstration of the skill he needs to perform, showing each stage of the technique, James will be provided with a mental image of what he should be doing. This means he will have something to recall mentally and copy when he tries to perform the skill physically.

Reorder the answer

1 Rearrange this student's answer into the most logical order by numbering each part.

5.4 Skills can be classified according to how the environment affects the skill, from basic skills to complex skills.

Order the skills below from closed to open. (4)

> **Hint**
> Remember: an open skill is one where the conditions are always changing; a closed skill is one that takes place in a stable and predictable environment.

- [ ] Footballer taking a penalty shot

- [ ] 100m sprint race

- [ ] Basketball free throw

- [ ] Netball player performing a chest pass to a team-mate in a game

2 Rearrange this student's answer into the most logical order by numbering each part.

5.5 SMART targets can be used to improve or optimise sports performance.

Giving an example, explain how the 'S' in SMART targets should be applied. (4)

> **Hint**
> It is important that answers to this type of question are in a logical order. Make sure you read your answer through from the start to check it makes sense.

- [ ] This means that the person knows exactly what the goal is.

- [ ] For example, a specific target could be 'I want to score 20 points in my next basketball game'.

- [ ] The person is then able to determine whether they have met their goal or not.

- [ ] The 'S' stands for Specific.

Complete the answer

1 Use the hint below to complete the student's answer so that it would be awarded 3 marks.

6.1 **Table 8** shows the typical body weights of males who compete at a high level in different sports.

Sport	Rugby	Judo	Horse racing	Football	Rowing	Gymnastics
Body weight (kg)	95	76	59	80	82	70

Table 8

(a) Using **Table 8**, explain which sport has the highest male body weight. (3)

Hint
The information you need to answer this question is found in **Table 8**, so look carefully at the data presented. Review the different body weights to see which one is the heaviest. Look at the sport the heaviest males take part in and try and work out why having a high body weight would be advantageous to that sport.

Had a go

Rugby players have the highest body weight. This is because ....

....

....

....

....

....

2 Use the hint below to complete the student's answer so that it would be awarded 3 marks.

(b) Using **Table 8**, explain which sport has the lowest male body weight. (3)

Hint
There are 3 marks available for this question. This answer identifies the sport correctly for the first mark. For the remaining 2 marks, you need to provide two points of explanation as to why having a low body weight is helpful to horse racing.

Had a go

Jockeys have the lowest body weight. This is because ....

....

....

....

....

....

Mark the answer

1 Use the mark scheme below to decide how many marks you would award the student's answer. Give reasons for your mark.

6.2 Angie is 52 years old. Her doctor has advised her to take part in jogging to improve the health of her skeletal system.

Explain **one** reason why Angie's doctor gave her this advice. (3)

Angie is at risk of getting osteoporosis, as she is getting older and this is something that can happen to women as they get older. This condition is where bones become brittle and more likely to break if she was to fall over. Jogging strengthens the bones, reducing the risk of osteoporosis.

Question	Answer	Mark
6.2	1 mark for identification of why jogging is beneficial for the skeletal system, and 1 mark for each linked explanation up to a total of 2 marks. For example: • Jogging helps to reduce the risk of osteoporosis (1). This is a skeletal problem for some some women as they get older due to a change in their hormone levels (1). It makes the bones more likely to fracture as the result of a fall (1). Or • Jogging stimulates the osteoclasts and osteoblasts (1), which increases the process of bone remodelling (1), which can make the bones stronger (1).	3

I would give this answer ..... out of 3 marks because ....

....

....

---

2 Use the mark scheme below to decide how many marks you would award the student's answer. Give reasons for your mark.

6.3 Weight-bearing exercises can improve skeletal bone health.

Giving an example, explain what is meant by weight-bearing exercise. (3)

Had a go

Weight-bearing exercise means you are carrying the weight of your body when you are exercising. An example would be cycling, as you are having to push the pedals with your legs.

Question	Answer	Mark
6.3	1 mark for identification of what weight-bearing exercise means, 1 mark for explanation, and 1 mark for an example. For example: • Weight-bearing exercise means the individual carries their own body weight while exercising (1). For example, when running (1) the person does not rely on any person or equipment to hold them up/support their weight in any way (1).	3

I would give this answer ..... out of 3 marks because ....

....

....

....

....

Complete the answer

1 Use the hint below to complete the answer.

7.1 Joshua is an athlete who competes in the long jump.

His coach has designed a training programme for him in preparation for a national championship in four months' time. His coach has used SMART targets to design the training programme.

Evaluate the need for the coach to use the 'S', the 'R' and the 'T' of the SMART targets in the training programme for Joshua.

(9)

> **Hint**
> You could take the following approach to answering this question:
> - **What?** Show knowledge and understanding of what 'S', 'R' and 'T' in SMART mean.
> - **How?** Explain how each target will help Joshua get ready for the championship.
> - **Why?** Discuss the impact of each target in helping Joshua prepare for the championship as a long-jump athlete.
>
> The student's answer for 'S' below contains the what, how and why, so is a complete answer for this part of the question.

Nearly there

'S' means 'specific' – that is, the target is clear so Joshua knows exactly what he is trying to achieve. This means focusing on a specific aspect of his long-jump technique during training, such as power for take-off. Training on power for take-off, for example using plyometrics, will help Joshua to jump high in the air in order to travel a longer distance. 'R' means realistic. The target has to be something that is

....

'T' means ....

Mark the answer

1 Draw lines to connect each of the marker's comments to the relevant part of the student's answer.

7.2 Sunita has a sedentary lifestyle. She decides to join a gym. As part of the gym's induction process, she takes part in some health and fitness tests.

Sunita then completes a six-week training programme, after which time she repeats the same health and fitness tests.

Table 9 shows the results of some of Sunita's health and fitness tests.

Health and fitness test	Before the training programme	After the training programme
Blood pressure	140/90	125/83
Body fat	Overweight	Healthy
Blood sugar level	High	Normal

Table 9

Evaluate the health benefits Sunita has gained from taking part in the six-week training programme.

(9)

> **Hint**
> A good plan for answering this question is to review each of the health fitness test results and compare the 'before training' with the 'after training' result. Think about what each health and fitness test measures and compare the results with the normal or 'healthy' ranges. Then think about the benefits to health of these changes, and any negatives if the results are not in the normal ranges.

The student has correctly identified that Sunita's blood sugar levels are high and described the health implications. However, the student has not given examples of how the programme has improved her blood sugar levels.

Nearly there

Sunita's blood pressure was high before the training programme.

This could be from high levels of cholesterol in the blood, which blocks

the blood vessels and increases the resistance to blood flow.

If left untreated, high blood pressure can lead to coronary heart

disease or a stroke. The training programme has reduced Sunita's

blood pressure so it is now normal, so there is less risk of her suffering

from ill health associated with high blood pressure. Sunita's body fat

levels were high as she was overweight. Excess fat around the heart

can lead to CHD or other health problems, such as diabetes and some

forms of cancer. Excess body fat also makes it harder to move around

and it may cause joint problems. Taking part in regular exercise has

caused Sunita to lose weight and she is now a healthy body weight.

This is because the exercise increased her energy output, so it was

higher than her energy input, resulting in a negative energy balance.

Because Sunita is now carrying less body weight, she will find it easier

to move around and is therefore more likely to maintain high activity

levels, which will help to further reduce the risk of CHD and some forms

of cancer. Sunita's high blood sugar levels indicate that she may have

diabetes, which can lead to blindness or kidney damage.

The student has correctly identified Sunita's high body fat levels and has given an accurate body composition category. The student has also correctly described health issues related to having excess body fat.

The student has correctly identified that Sunita's blood pressure values were too high. They have also explained why this may be and the health consequences of this.

The student has explained the impact of Sunita's training programme on reducing her body fat levels and the health benefits.

The student has explained the impact of the training programme in reducing blood pressure, and the health benefits of this.

Mark the answer

1   Use the mark scheme below to decide how many marks you would award the student's answer on the previous page.

7.2   Evaluate the health benefits Sunita has gained from taking part in the six-week training programme.   (9)

Question	Indicative content	Mark
7.2	**Blood pressure:** • Sunita had high blood pressure before the training programme. • This can be from high levels of cholesterol in the blood, which blocks the blood vessels. • High blood pressure can lead to CHD or a stroke. • The training programme has reduced blood pressure to normal levels, so there is less risk of ill health associated with high blood pressure. **Body fat:** • Sunita was overweight, which meant she had excessive body fat. • Excess fat around the heart can lead to CHD. • Excess body fat meant she was heavier, so will have found it harder to move/ which may have negatively affected her joints. • Regular exercise led to a negative energy balance and weight loss. • She will now find it easier to move around and is therefore more likely to maintain high activity levels. There is also a reduced risk of CHD. **Blood sugar level:** • High blood sugar level indicates diabetes. • High levels of sugar in the blood damage blood vessels. • If left untreated it can lead to blindness/kidney damage. • Regular exercise helps to regulate insulin levels, which has resulted in normal blood sugar levels. • Reduction in or no further damage to blood vessels means less likely to suffer from health issues associated with diabetes.	9

Level	Mark	Descriptor
1	1–3	• Demonstrates isolated elements of knowledge and understanding, with limited technical language used. • Limited attempt to apply knowledge to question context. • Generic assertions may be presented.
2	4–6	• Demonstrates isolated elements of knowledge and understanding, with limited technical language used. • Limited attempt to apply knowledge to question context. • Generic assertions may be presented.
3	7–9	• Demonstrates accurate knowledge and understanding throughout, including appropriate use of technical language. • Applies detailed knowledge to question context throughout. • Reaches a valid and well-reasoned conclusion supported by relevant evidence.

I would give this answer .... out of 9 marks because ....

....

....

....

....

....

....

....

Complete the answer

1 Use the hint below to complete the student's answer so that it would be awarded 6 marks.

8.1 The London Paralympic Games were held in 2012 and widely considered a successful event.

Figure 10 shows participation in sport and physical activity by people with disabilities at a leisure centre near central London from 2000 to 2016.

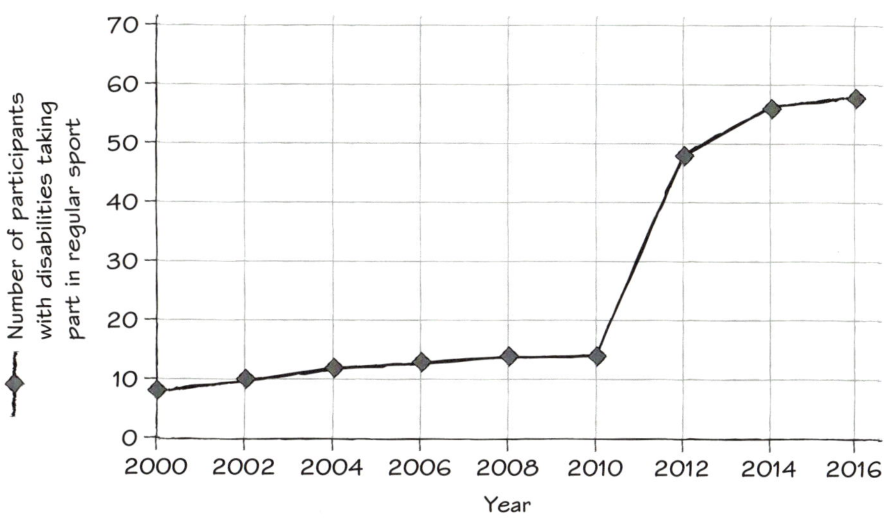

Figure 10

Explain **two** reasons why participation in sport and physical activity by people with disabilities increased from 2012 onwards.

(6)

> **Hint**
> An improved student answer might mention the following points:
> - There was a significant increase in participation in 2012.
> - The London Paralympic Games in 2012 inspired people with disabilities to take part in sport and physical activity.
> - There were more sport/leisure facilities for people with disabilities after the 2012 London Paralympic Games.

....

....

....

Had a go

The London Paralympic Games may have inspired people with disabilities to take part in sport

....

....

....

....

....

....

....

Improve the answer

1 Use the hint below to write an improved answer that would be awarded 3 marks.

8.2 Tegan is a shot-put thrower. She takes part in weight training to improve her shot-put throwing performance.

Explain which macronutrient is most important to help Tegan's body recover from weight training. (3)

Had a go

Protein should be eaten.

> **Hint**
> The student has correctly stated the macronutrient that should be consumed. For full marks they would need to explain why it is required to help the body recover from weight training.

2 Use the hint below to write an improved answer that would be awarded 3 marks.

8.3 In some sports, participants can exhibit gamesmanship.

Using a sporting example, explain what is meant by gamesmanship. (3)

Had a go

Gamesmanship is where a participant tries to gain an unfair advantage over their opposition by pushing the boundaries of the rules.

> **Hint**
> The student has provided an excellent definition of gamesmanship. To gain full marks, they need to give a sports-related example with an explanation of how this shows gamesmanship.

Mark the answer

1 Draw lines to connect each of the marker's comments to the relevant part of the student's answer.

8.4 Aisha is 19 years old and suffers from mild depression. She lives on her own and does not have many friends. Her doctor tells her that her physical and mental health would improve if she took part in group-based exercise classes at the local community centre.

Explain which **two** other types of health will be improved from Aisha's participation in group-based exercise classes. **(6)**

> **Hint**
> Always read all the information you are given as part of a question very carefully. Here, the information identifies two types of health: physical and mental. But the question then asks you to write about two 'other types' of health, so you must choose two other types of health to write about. If you write about 'physical' and 'mental' health, you will gain no marks.

The student has given a reason why taking part in physical exercise improves emotional health.

The student has identified a different type of health correctly.

1 Aisha's emotional health will improve. This is because participation in exercise will increase the production of endorphins. Endorphins are mood-enhancing hormones and relieve feelings of depression.

2 Aisha's social health will improve as she will meet new people at the local exercise classes. She could form new friendships from seeing these people on a regular basis, which will mean she feels less isolated socially.

The student has explained how forming new friendships will help Aisha's social health.

The student has given a reason why taking part in physical exercise improves social health.

The student has explained how physical activity helps to reduce depression.

The student has identified a second type of health correctly.

2 Now use the mark scheme below to decide how many marks you would award the student's answer above. Give reasons for your mark.

Question	Answer	Mark
8.4	1 mark for identification for each type of health and up to 2 marks for each related explanatory point. Up to 3 marks for responses related to each type of health improvement. • Emotional health will increase (1) as participation in exercise increases the production of endorphins (1), which are mood-enhancing hormones and relieve feelings of depression (1). • Social health will improve (1) because she will meet new people at a group exercise class who could become friends over time (1), meaning she is less socially isolated (1).	6

I would award the student's answer   marks because ....

....

....

....

Complete the question

1 Complete the question by adding **two** multiple-choice options. Make sure one is correct.

9.1 Which **one** of the following is a negative impact on a person's health from excessive alcohol consumption? **(1)**

> **Hint**
> Multiple-choice answers always contain believable answers. Make sure your incorrect option really tests a student's understanding of the health effects of alcohol on the body.

☐ **A** ....

☐ **B** Bronchitis

☑ **C** ....

☐ **D** High cholesterol

2 Complete the question by adding **two** multiple-choice options. Make sure one is correct.

9.2 Which **one** of the following is the term given for high blood pressure? **(1)**

☑ **A** ....

☐ **B** Hypoglycaemia

☐ **C** Hypotension

☐ **D** ....

3 Complete the question by adding **two** multiple-choice options. Make sure one is correct.

9.3 Which **one** of the following is a type of feedback that is given at the time of the performance? **(1)**

> **Hint**
> When answering this question, remember that all the multiple-choice options have to name a type of feedback.

☐ **A** Extrinsic

☐ **B** ....

☐ **C** Intrinsic

☑ **D** ....

Find the answer

1 Use the mark scheme below to find the student's answer that would be awarded 2 marks. Choose **A**, **B** or **C**. Explain your choice.

9.4 (a) Explain **one** advantage to a magazine company of using a well-known sports performer to advertise its new product. **(2)**

Question	Answer	Mark
9.4 (a)	1 mark for identification of an advantage and 1 mark for a related expansion. For example: • Using a well-known sports performer will increase awareness of the product (1) so more people are likely to buy the magazine, which will increase the company's profits (1). Accept any other appropriate responses.	2

(b) Explain **one** disadvantage to a magazine company of using a well-known sports performer to advertise its new product. **(2)**

Question	Answer	Mark
9.4 (b)	1 mark for identification of an advantage and 1 mark for each related expansion. • The sports performer may take part in inappropriate/illegal behaviour (1), which would make people not want to buy the magazine because it is associated with the performer's negative behaviour (1). Accept any other appropriate responses.	2

A
(a) It will make more people aware of the product, which will affect sales.
(b) The role model may be in the news, which would make people not want to buy the product.

B
(a) More people will be aware of the product so there is more chance that more people will buy it, so the company can make more money.
(b) The role model may take illegal recreational drugs, which would make people associate the magazine with that person's drug taking and stop them buying it.

C
(a) More people will know about the product as they will know the role model and think it must be a good product if they are advertising it.
(b) The role model may get worse at their sport so people would associate the magazine with playing poorly at sport.

Answer .... would be awarded 4 marks because ....

....

....

....

For part (b) the student has ....

....

....

Complete the question

1 Use the hint below and the student's answer to complete the question.

> **9.5** Which **one** of the following foods is highest in the macronutrient .... ? **(1)**
>
> > **Hint**
> > Options A, B and D are foods with high levels of carbohydrate and are all incorrect options, so the answer is **not** carbohydrate. Which other macronutrient is found in option C?
>
> ☐ **A** Pasta   ☑ **C** Cream
>
> ☐ **B** Bread   ☐ **D** Rice

2 Use the hint below and the student's answer to complete the question.

> **9.6** Which **one** of the following is the technical term for high .... ? **(1)**
>
> > **Hint**
> > The four options are all health conditions and the question contains the term 'high', so consider which health condition means that a particular measure of health is high.
>
> ☐ **A** Cirrhosis of the liver   ☐ **C** Osteoporosis
>
> ☑ **B** Hypertension   ☐ **D** Hypotension

3 Use the hint below and the student's answer to complete the question.

> **9.7** A trampoline coach uses a harness to help participants learn how to do a somersault on the trampoline. **(1)**
>
> Which type of .... is this?
>
> > **Hint**
> > Look carefully at the four answers to work out the question: what are they all types of?
>
> ☐ **A** Visual   ☐ **C** Manual
>
> ☐ **B** Verbal   ☑ **D** Mechanical

Mark the answer

1 Use the mark scheme below to decide how many marks you would award the student's answer. Give reasons for your mark.

10.1 **Figure 11** shows participation in different sports related to socio-economic group (SEG).

High SEG indicates high personal wealth and low SEG indicates low personal wealth.

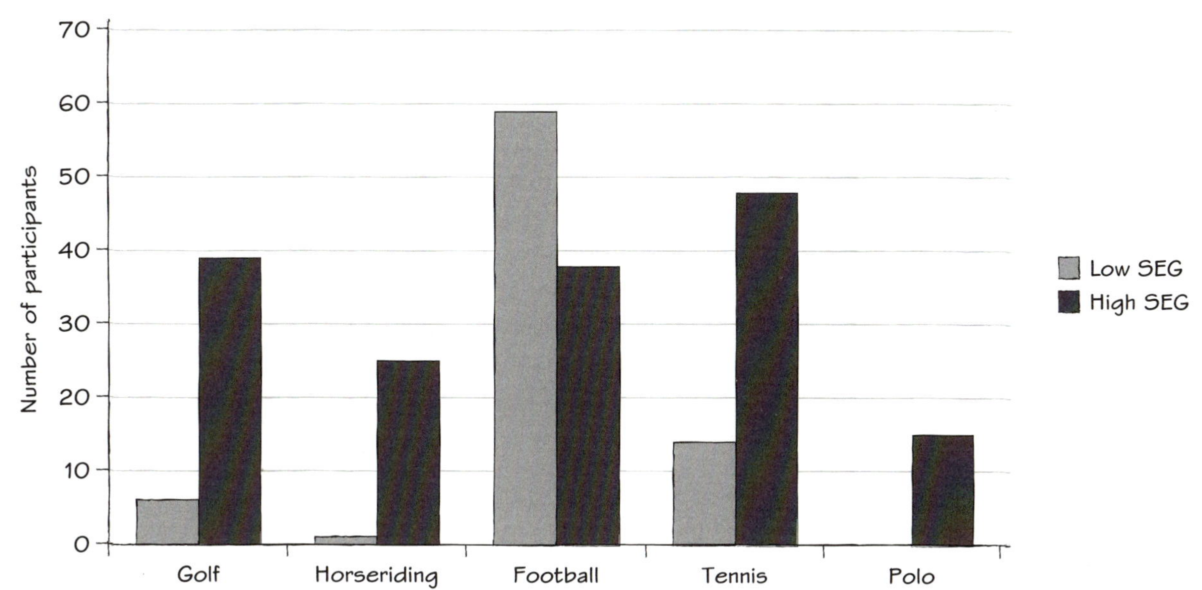

Figure 11

(a) Using the data in **Figure 11**, identify which sport has the lowest participation rates for the low SEG. **(1)**

Polo

(b) Give **one** reason to justify your answer to Question 10.1 (a). **(2)**

People in the low SEG do not have enough money spare after having paid their bills and living costs to then be able to have the money to take part in polo, as this sport needs a horse, which costs a lot of money to own or hire.

Question	Answer	Mark
10.1 (a)	Polo	1
10.1 (b)	People in the low SEG do not have much disposable income available (1) and would not be able to afford to take part in polo as owning a horse costs a lot of money (1).	2

I would award answer 10.1 (a)   out of 1 mark because

I would award answer 10.1 (b)   out of 2 marks because

Complete the answer

1 Complete the student's answer so that it would be awarded 3 marks.

10.2 Give **three** examples of how physical health can be improved by participation in sport and physical activity. **(3)**

> **Hint**
> Remember: physical health is related to your body and can include body composition, so your answer could include factors related to the ratio of body fat to muscle mass.

Had a go

1 Improve fitness ....

2 ....

3 ....

2 Complete the student's answer so that it would be awarded 3 marks.

10.3 Rayan is a marathon runner and is training to compete in the London marathon.

Explain why it is important for Rayan to consume drinks while running the marathon. **(3)**

> **Hint**
> The student has clearly stated why Rayan should drink while running the marathon. You now need to explain why Rayan may lose fluids while running and describe why it is important for him to avoid this, for example by giving an example of a possible negative effect of dehydration.

Had a go

Rayan should drink so that he stays hydrated while running the marathon. ....

....

....

....

....

....

....

....

....

....

....

Mark the answer

1 Use the mark scheme below to decide how many marks you would award the student's answers. Give reasons for your marks.

10.4 Dilraj coaches beginners' volleyball for children aged 11 to 12 years old.

She coaches distributed practice and massed practice in her coaching sessions.

> **Hint**
> The key information in the question is the type of participant Dilraj is working with: they are beginners and they are children. You need to work out how the type of practice is going to help to support these participants in learning a new skill.

(a) Explain **one** advantage of using distributed practice for beginners' volleyball coaching sessions. (2)

Distributed practice means there are lots of different things going on in the coaching session, which helps beginners to do lots of different things. This is good as it can get boring just focusing on one type of technique or skill in a session.

Question	Answer	Mark
10.4 (a)	Distributed practice involves lots of changes in the activity (1), which will help to reduce the boredom that may be experienced by beginners learning a new sport (1).	2

I would award this answer .... out of 2 marks because

(b) Explain **one** advantage of using massed practice for beginners' volleyball coaching sessions. (2)

This type of practice means all the children do the same thing, which helps them get better.

Question	Answer	Mark
10.4 (b)	Massed practice gives the children plenty of time to focus on the skill they need to learn (1), which is good as the children will be learning skills that they have not performed before (1).	2

I would award this answer .... out of 2 marks because

> After I have completed my answer to a question, I always read it back to myself to make sure it makes sense and to check that I have used the correct PE terminology.

Improve the answer

1 Use the hint below to write an improved answer that would be awarded 3 marks.

11.1 Figure 12 shows the golden triangle that links sport, sponsorship and media.

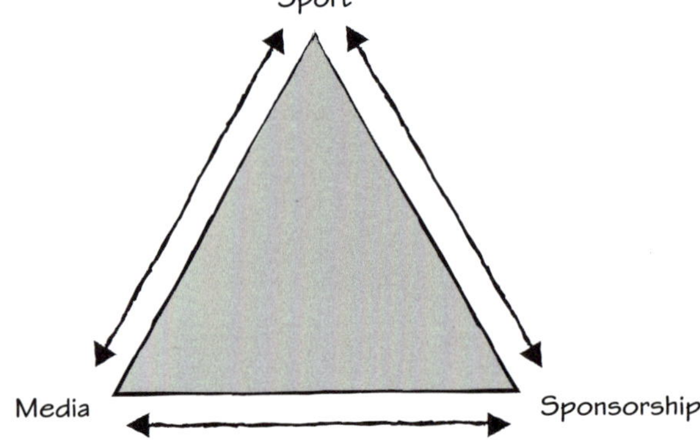

Figure 12

(a) Explain **one** advantage to sport of sponsorship. **(3)**

> **Hint**
> This answer correctly states how sponsorship is advantageous to sport. To get full marks, two linked points of explanation must now be given about why having an increased income is beneficial to sport. For example, you could consider what the money could be used for to help improve the performance of the players.

Had a go

Sponsorship can increase the amount of income available for a sports team.

....

....

....

(b) Explain **one** disadvantage of sponsorship on sport. **(3)**

> **Hint**
> This answer clearly states that sponsorship could be a disadvantage to a sports team if the sponsoring brand has a negative image. To get full marks, a clear reason must now be given as to why this may be a disadvantage for a sports team, for example if the brand product is considered to be unhealthy or if the company behind the brand has unethical working practices.

Had a go

Sponsorship can be a disadvantage if a sporting team is associated with a brand that has a negative public image.

....

....

....

> I found it useful to look at and practise as many exam questions as possible before the exam. Doing this really helped my understanding of how to answer them successfully.

Mark the answer

1 Draw lines to connect each of the marker's comments to the relevant part of the student's answer.

11.2 Sammy is a single mum with two children, aged 1 and 3 years old. She is not able to drive and lives in a small village with no sports facilities. The nearest sports facilities are in a town four miles away.

Sammy's doctor has diagnosed her with type 2 diabetes and she now requires insulin injections to manage this condition. Her doctor also advised Sammy to try to lose weight and take part in physical activity.

Sammy would like to take part in more physical activity, but there are a number of barriers she needs to overcome in order to participate in sport.

Evaluate **three** barriers impacting on Sammy's ability to participate in regular sport and physical activity. **(9)**

The student has correctly identified availability as a barrier to Sammy's participation, using information from the question well.

Nearly there

The main barriers impacting on Sammy's ability to participate in sport and physical activity are access, time and health problems.

Access is a barrier as Sammy lives in a village that does not have any sports facilities. She is not able to drive, so would need to get public transport to her nearest sports facilities, but there may not be any bus routes or a train in her village that could take her to the nearest leisure centre.

Availability is also a barrier, as Sammy has two children to look after and does not have a partner to support her in this. This means she can't take part in sport or physical activity unless she can find someone to look after her children. The local leisure centre may have a crèche, which would mean she could take part in sport or physical activity while her children are being looked after at the crèche.

Health problems are also a barrier, as Sammy has just been diagnosed with diabetes. She may feel worried that if she does take part in sport or physical activity the people running the sessions may not know how to support a person with this condition and she may become unwell when participating.

Each one of these barriers will have an equal impact on Sammy's ability to participate in sport and physical activity.

Solutions for Sammy to resolve the issues with availability have been suggested but the question does not ask for this, so this part of the answer would gain no credit.

The student has correctly identified access as a barrier to Sammy's participation in regular sport and physical activity, supported by information from the question.

The student has attempted a conclusion but has not reached an overall judgement about The student has provided a conclusion with an overall judgment that each barrier has an equal impact which matches their response.

The student has correctly identified Sammy's health issues as a barrier to her participation, and has given some sound reasons why they are a barrier.

The student has given some sound reasons for why access is a barrier to Sammy participating in sport regularly.

The student has explained why availability is a barrier to Sammy participating in sport regularly.

Mark the answer

1 Use the mark scheme below to decide how many marks you would award the student's answer on the previous page. Give reasons for your mark.

11.3 Evaluate **three** barriers that are impacting on Sammy's ability to participate in regular sport and physical activity. **(9)**

Question	Indicative content	Mark
11.3	Each one of the following barriers will have an impact on Sammy's ability to participate in sport and physical activity, and needs to be addressed. • Access: the village does not have any sports facilities; Sammy cannot drive so relies on public transport; there may not be any bus or railway routes to the nearest leisure centre. • Availability: she has two children to look after; she is a single mum so has no partner help look after the children. • Health problems: she has type 2 diabetes, which is a health condition that can make participation in sport difficult; type 2 diabetes is associated with obesity and problems with maintaining blood sugar levels, both of which may limit her ability to participate in sport; she may worry that sports leaders may not be qualified to support her if she becomes unwell when participating.	9

Level	Marks	Descriptor
1	1–3	• Demonstrates isolated elements of knowledge and understanding, with limited technical language used. • Limited attempt to apply knowledge to question context. • Generic assertions may be presented.
2	4–6	• Demonstrates mostly accurate knowledge and understanding, including appropriate use of technical language in places. • Applies knowledge to question context. • Attempts at drawing conclusion, with some support from relevant evidence.
3	7–9	• Demonstrates accurate knowledge and understanding throughout, including appropriate use of technical language. • Applies detailed knowledge to question context throughout. • Reaches a valid and well-reasoned conclusion, supported by relevant evidence.

Nearly there

I would give this student's answer ______ out of 9 marks because ....

....

....

....

....

....

....

....

....

....

....

....

Complete the answer

1 Complete the student's answer so that it would be awarded 2 marks.

12.1 Table 10 shows Olympic doping cases from 1968 to 2010 by sport.

Sport	Number of doping cases reported
Weightlifting	36
Athletics (track and field)	28
Cross-country skiing	12
Equestrian	8
Ice hockey, wrestling	6
Cycling	5
Biathlon, modern pentathlon, volleyball	3
Baseball, gymnastics, judo, rowing, swimming, shooting	3
Alpine skiing, basketball, boxing, canoeing, sailing	1

Table 10

(a) Using **Table 10**, identify the **two** activities with the lowest number of reported doping cases. (2)

> **Hint**
> In **Table 10** there are a selection of sports with the lowest number of reported doping cases, so you could choose any two sports from this selection to gain the marking points available.

Nearly there

Alpine skiing,

2 Complete the student's answer so that it would be awarded 3 marks.

(b) Explain the most likely type of performance-enhancing drug to be taken by cross-country skiers. (3)

> **Hint**
> The student has correctly identified the performance-enhancing drug most likely to be taken by cross-country skiers. To complete the answer, you need to explain the effect of EPO on the body and give a reason why cross-country skiers would need this effect to help them with their sport.

Had a go

The most likely drug to be taken by cross-country skiers would be EPO as this

Mark the answer

1 Use the mark scheme below to decide how many marks you would award the student's answer. Give reasons for your mark.

12.2 A sedentary lifestyle can have negative health consequences.

Give **one** example of a risk to long-term health from leading a sedentary lifestyle. (1)

> **Hint**
> A risk is anything that could potentially harm you. This question is asking you to consider how a sedentary lifestyle could potentially harm a person's health over the long term. 'Sedentary' means not taking part in physical activity.

Had a go

One risk is increased muscle tone.

I find it really helpful to underline the key words in the question. It helps me focus on what I have to do.

Question	Answer	Mark
12.2	Any one from the following list: • depression (1) • diabetes (1) • coronary heart disease (CHD) (1) • increased risk of osteoporosis (1). • high blood pressure (1)	1

I would award this student's answer   out of 1 mark because

....

....

....

2 Use the mark scheme below to decide how many marks you would award the student's answer. Give reasons for your mark.

12.3 Personal factors such as gender can affect participation rates in sport and physical activity.

State **three** other personal factors that can affect participation rates. (3)

Had a go

1   How old they are   2   Their ethnicity   3   If they are male or female

Question	Answer	Mark
12.3	Any three from the following list: • age (1) • ethnicity (1) • socio-economic group (1) • disability (1).	3

I would award this student's answer   out of 3 marks because

....

....

....

....

Find the answer

1 Use the mark scheme to find the student's answer that would be awarded 2 marks. Explain your choice.

12.4 Alex is a basketball player and uses mental rehearsal before she takes a free throw shot in a game.

Explain **one** way in which mental rehearsal will improve Alex's free throw shots in a basketball game. (2)

> **Hint**
> There are 2 marks available for this question. For the first mark, you need to identify a type of mental rehearsal that will improve Alex's free throw shots. To gain the second mark, you need to show application by describing how that mental rehearsal will help improve her free throw shots.

A It will give Alex time to think about the shot so she has a better chance of getting the ball in the basket.

B Mental rehearsal will give Alex the time to see herself performing the shot, which could help reduce any stress she may have, allowing her to just concentrate on taking the free shot.

C This will help her to not hear the crowd, which may be making noises and putting her off.

Question	Answer	Mark
12.4	1 mark for an example of mental rehearsal: • It will allow Alex to visualise the shot (1). 1 mark for application to free throw shots in basketball. For example: • It will reduce her stress/allow her to focus on the technique/allow her to block out the noises from the spectators, so she is less likely to make an error during the shot (1).	2

Answer .... would be awarded 2 marks because ....

....

....

....

....

....

....

> When revising, I found looking at good and poor answers to exam questions really helped me understand what the examiner is looking for.

Complete the question

1 Complete the question by adding **two** multiple-choice options. Make sure one is correct.

12.5 SMART targets are used to improve sports performance.

Which **one** of the following is the correct term for the 'T' in SMART targets? (1)

☐ **A** Time-measured

☑ **B** …………………………………………

☐ **C** Type

☐ **D** …………………………………………

> **Hint**
> Multiple-choice answers always contain believable answers. Make sure your incorrect option really tests a student's knowledge of what the letters in the acronym 'SMART' stand for.

2 Complete the question by adding **two** multiple-choice options. Make sure one is correct.

12.6 SMART targets are used to improve sports performance.

Which **one** of the following is the correct term for the 'M' in SMART targets? (1)

☐ **A** …………………………………………

☐ **B** Measured

☐ **C** Medium

☑ **D** …………………………………………

3 Complete the question by adding **two** multiple-choice options. Make sure one is correct.

12.7 SMART targets are used to improve sports performance.

Which **one** of the following is the correct term for the 'R' in SMART targets? (1)

☑ **A** …………………………………………

☐ **B** Reliable

☐ **C** …………………………………………

☐ **D** Regular

Mark the answer

1 Draw lines to connect each of the marker's comments to the relevant part of the student's answer.

13.1 (a) Abbie is learning how to perform the triple jump. When she trains, her coach provides feedback to her while she is taking part in the jump.

Explain **one** advantage of the coach giving Abbie feedback while she is in the process of completing the triple jump. (3)

Hint
For this question you need to identify the type of feedback the coach provides while Abbie completes the triple jump. You then need to think about why delivering feedback in this format is beneficial to the performer when they are specifically taking part in the triple jump.

Nailed it!

The coach is giving Abbie concurrent feedback, which is good as it takes place when the person is performing the skill. This helps Abbie to remember an important part of the technique as she practises it.

The student has described how the feedback has been used.

The student has successfully explained why this type of feedback is advantageous.

The correct type of feedback has been identified.

2 Draw lines to connect each of the marker's comments to the relevant part of the student's answer.

(b) At the end of the triple-jump practice, the coach gives Abbie more feedback on how she performed.

Explain **one** advantage of the coach giving Abbie feedback once the triple-jump skill has been performed. (3)

Nearly there

This type of feedback is good because it gives the athlete information about the end result of their performance.

This is good because the performer can have time to focus on the feedback and relate this to what they have done, and they can learn from this how to improve their skill.

The student has demonstrated knowledge of why this type of feedback is used.

The student has successfully explained the advantage of this type of feedback in relation to how it is used to improve performance.

The student has failed to identify the type of feedback being given – they have only said it is 'good'. This part of the answer does not gain a mark.

Improve the answer

1 Use the hint below to write an improved answer that would be awarded 3 marks.

13.2 Ann is 56 years old and has been advised by her doctor that she is at risk of osteoporosis.

Explain which micronutrient is most important to help reduce the risk of osteoporosis. (3)

Had a go

Osteoporosis is a disease where the bones become brittle.

Hint

The student has correctly identified what osteoporosis is. However, the type of micronutrient has not been given – this needs to be included to get the second marking point. There also needs to be an explanation of what the micronutrient does to help reduce the risk of osteoporosis.

2 Use the hint below to write an improved answer that would be awarded 2 marks.

13.3 Tyrone eats a diet that contains very little fibre. Explain **one** health concern linked to eating low levels of fibre. (2)

Had a go

Fibre helps to prevent constipation. You can find it in foods such as bran flakes.

Hint

The student has correctly identified a health concern linked to not eating enough fibre (constipation), but then goes on to describe a food high in fibre. This is not required by the question. To gain the second marking point, an explanation of how fibre helps prevent constipation needs to be given.

3 Use the hint below to write an improved answer that would be awarded 2 marks.

13.4 Jill smokes cigarettes. Explain **one** health concern associated with smoking cigarettes. (2)

Had a go

Jill is at risk of suffering from emphysema. She may also develop lung cancer.

Hint

Two health concerns have been identified but the question only asks for one. For the second mark, an explanation is required of how smoking cigarettes can cause one health concern.

Complete the answer

1 Complete the student's answer so that it would be awarded 3 marks.

13.5 **Figure 13** shows the percentage of overall macro and micronutrient intake that should be consumed on a daily basis.

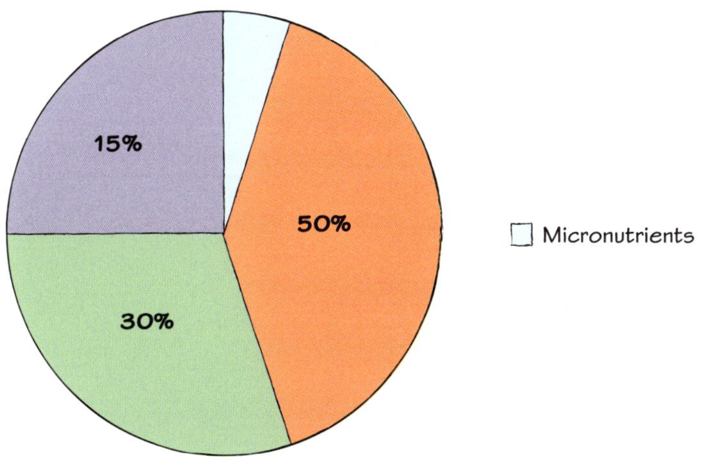

Figure 13

(a) Complete the key below to identify the macronutrients represented by the red, green and purple areas in the pie chart.

(3)

> **Hint**
> Think about which macronutrient we need the highest quantities of on a daily basis.

Had a go

	Carbohydrates	
		(1)
		(1)
		(1)

2 Complete the student's answer so that it would be awarded 2 marks.

(b) We only need very small quantities of micronutrients in our diet.
State **two** types of micronutrient.

(2)

> **Hint**
> Make sure you identify the two types of micronutrient in your response, rather than giving examples of each type of micronutrient.

Had a go

Vitamins and ....

Complete the question

1 Use the hint and the student's answer below to complete the question.

13.6 Brian is a long-distance runner. He has been told he should eat foods that are high in ....

Identify **two** different types of food that Brian could eat. (2)

Nailed it!

1 Rice ....

2 Pasta ....

Hint
Two types of food are identified in the student's answer. What macronutrient are these foods high in?

2 Use the student's answer below to complete the question.

13.7 Sunita is a weightlifter. To help her increase muscle mass, she has been told she should eat foods high in

....

Identify **two** different types of food Sunita could eat. (2)

Nailed it!

1 Chicken ....

2 Fish ....

3 Use the hint and student's answer below to complete the question.

13.8 Identify **two** functions of .... (2)

Nailed it!

1 Storage of vitamin A ....

2 Insulation ....

Hint
Two functions of a macronutrient are identified in the student's answer. What macronutrient has these functions?

I always follow a fail-safe method when answering exam questions: I read the question, then look at the number of marks available, then read the question again and decide how many points I need to make for each part of the question. This approach really helped me get my timings right in the exam.

Complete the question

1 Complete the question by adding **two** multiple-choice options. Make sure one is correct.

13.9 (a) **Figure 14** shows the percentage of people within different body-weight groups who live in Hobbyshire and have coronary heart disease.

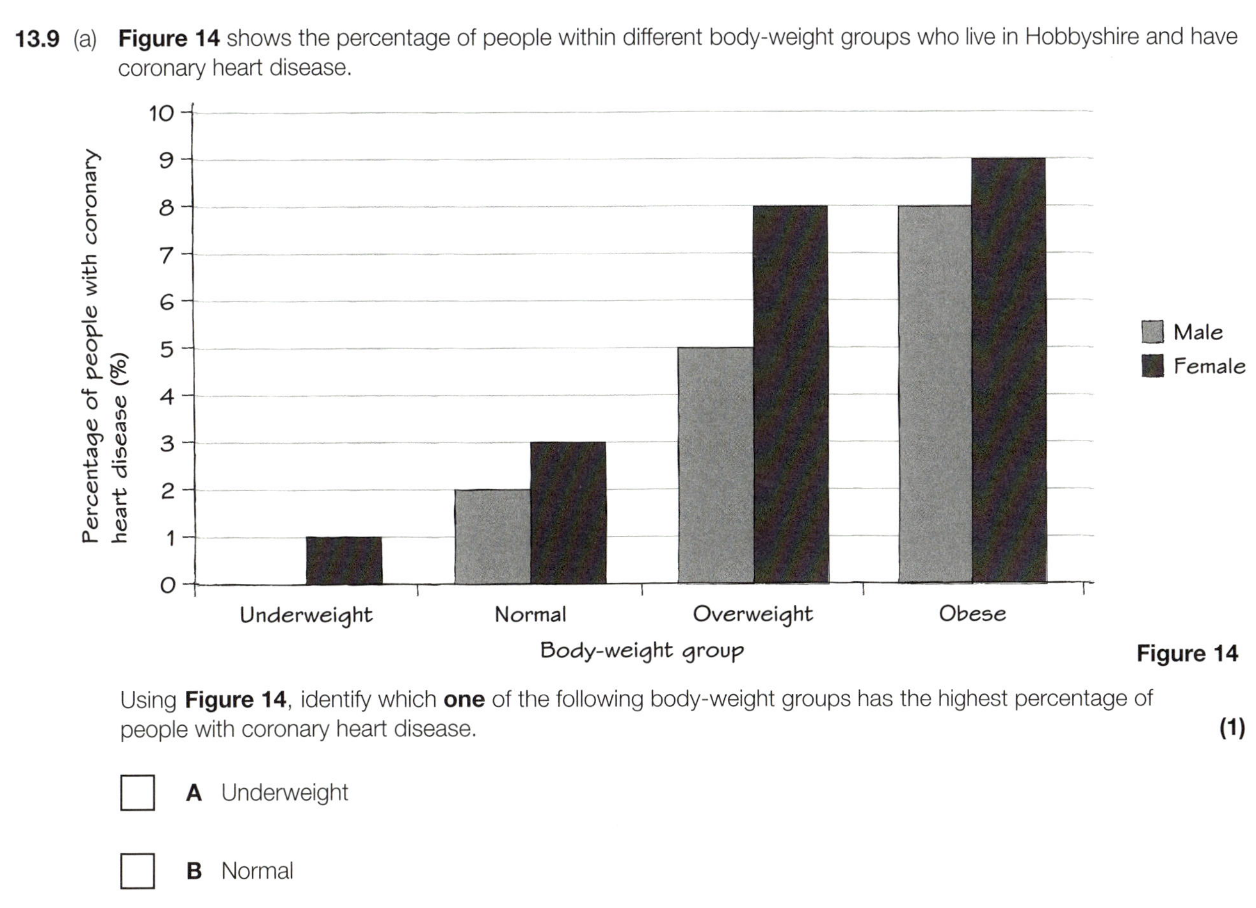

Using **Figure 14**, identify which **one** of the following body-weight groups has the highest percentage of people with coronary heart disease. **(1)**

☐ **A** Underweight

☐ **B** Normal

☐ **C** ....

☑ **D** ....

2 Use the hint and the student's answer below to complete the question.

(b) Using **Figure 14**, identify the body-weight group where the percentage of females with coronary heart

disease is .... **(1)**

> **Hint**
> This question is asking which body-weight group of females has a given percentage of coronary heart disease. To work out the percentage figure in the question, you will need to:
> • use the information in the answer to identify the correct group
> • use the graph to work out the percentage of females in this group.
> Take care: check that you are looking at the percentage of women in that group and not men.

Nailed it!

Overweight ....

Answers

Where an example answer is given, this is not necessarily the only correct response. In most cases, there is a range of responses that can gain full marks.

In questions that have more than one correct answer, you will see the (Suggested answer) stamp.

Complete the answer

1 Complete the student's answer so that it would be awarded 4 marks.

1.1 Muscles work with the skeleton to bring about specific sporting movements.

Complete **Table 1** by:

(a) identifying **two** different muscle fibre types

(b) stating a characteristic of each fibre type. (4)

Hint
The number of marks available is a good guide to how many points you need to make in your answer. For example, there are 4 marks available here, which generally means that four separate points or items are required in your response.

(Suggested answer)

(a) Muscle fibre type	(b) Characteristic
Type I (1)	This fibre is able to contract for long periods of time without fatiguing. (1)
Type IIx (1)	This fibre is able to contract with very high force. (1)

(Suggested answer)

Table 1

I always follow a fail-safe method when answering exam questions: I read the question, then look at the number of marks available, then read the question again and decide how many points I need to make for each part of the question. This approach really helped me get my timings right in the exam.

2 Complete the student's answer so that it would be awarded 4 marks.

1.2 Blood vessels form part of the cardiovascular system.

Complete **Table 2** by:

(a) stating **one** structure of each blood vessel

(b) stating **one** function of each blood vessel. (4)

(Suggested answer)

Blood vessel	(a) Structure	(b) Function
Vein	Contains valves (1)	Returns blood to the heart (1)
Artery	Has strong elastic walls (1)	Takes blood away from the heart (1)

(Suggested answer)

Table 2

Improve the answer

1 Write an improved answer to the question below. Use the hint to make sure your answer achieves the highest possible mark.

1.3 Jackie takes part in a cross-country run.

Table 3 shows Jackie's tidal volume at rest and during her cross-country run.

Tidal volume at rest	500 ml
Tidal volume during cross-country run	800 ml

Table 3

Using the data in **Table 3**, explain the difference in Jackie's tidal volume at rest and during her cross-country run. (3)

Had a go

Jackie's tidal volume increases from 500 ml at rest to 800 ml while taking part in a cross-country run. This is because she needs to get more air into her body.

Hint
This student's answer would gain 1 mark for successfully explaining the difference, but would receive no further marks for explanation. To improve the student's answer, you need to explain why the increase happens, using the correct scientific terms such as 'oxygen' and 'aerobic energy system'. Remember: use the data from the table in your answer.

Jackie's tidal volume increases from 500 ml at rest to (Suggested answer) 800 ml while taking part in a cross-country run. This is because she needs to take in more oxygen per breath while she is running. The extra oxygen is used to help produce energy through the aerobic energy system.

2 Write an improved answer to the question below. Use the hint to make sure your answer achieves the highest possible mark.

1.4 Alveoli are located in the lungs and are the site of gaseous exchange.

Explain how **one** structure of alveoli aids gaseous exchange. (2)

Had a go

Alveoli have semi-permeable membranes and are surrounded by capillaries, which helps with gaseous exchange.

Hint
In this student's answer, although two structures in the lungs have been identified, the student will gain just 1 mark because the question asks for only one structure to be explained. The student has provided no explanation of how either structure helps with gaseous exchange.

Alveoli have semi-permeable membranes, which means (Suggested answer) oxygen and carbon dioxide are able to diffuse into and out of them. This supports gaseous exchange.

Complete the question

1 Complete the question by adding **two** multiple-choice options. Make sure one is correct.

2.1 (a) Which one of the following correctly states the role of tendons? (1)

Hint
Multiple-choice answers always contain believable answers. Make sure your incorrect option really tests a student's understanding of the role of tendons.

- [ ] A Join bone to bone
- [✓] C Join muscle to bone
- [ ] B Join muscle to muscle
- [ ] D Join muscle to cartilage (Suggested answer)

2 Complete the question by adding **two** multiple-choice options. Make sure one is correct.

(b) Which one of the following is the correct classification of the neck joint? (1)

Hint
When answering this question, remember that all the multiple-choice options have to name an actual type of joint rather than being made-up terms.

- [ ] A Hinge
- [ ] C Ball and socket
- [✓] B Pivot
- [ ] D Saddle (Suggested answer)

3 Complete the question by adding **two** multiple-choice options.

(c) Which one of the following is **not** a function of the skeleton? (1)

Hint
Watch out! The question asks students to identify which option is incorrect, so you need to write in two **correct** functions of the skeleton.

(Suggested answer)

- [ ] A Protects vital organs
- [ ] C Produces platelets
- [ ] B Stores calcium
- [✓] D Stores vitamin A

Mark the answer

1 Use the mark scheme below to decide how many marks you would award the student's answer. Give reasons for your decision.

2.2 **Figure 1** shows a person performing a squat using a barbell.

Examine the antagonistic muscle action that takes place at the right knee and right hip as the person rises from the squat position to standing. (6)

Hint
To gain the full 6 marks available for this question, you must use technical terminology in your answer. For example, you should use the term 'extend' rather than 'straighten', and you should name the joints where movement in the leg occurs.

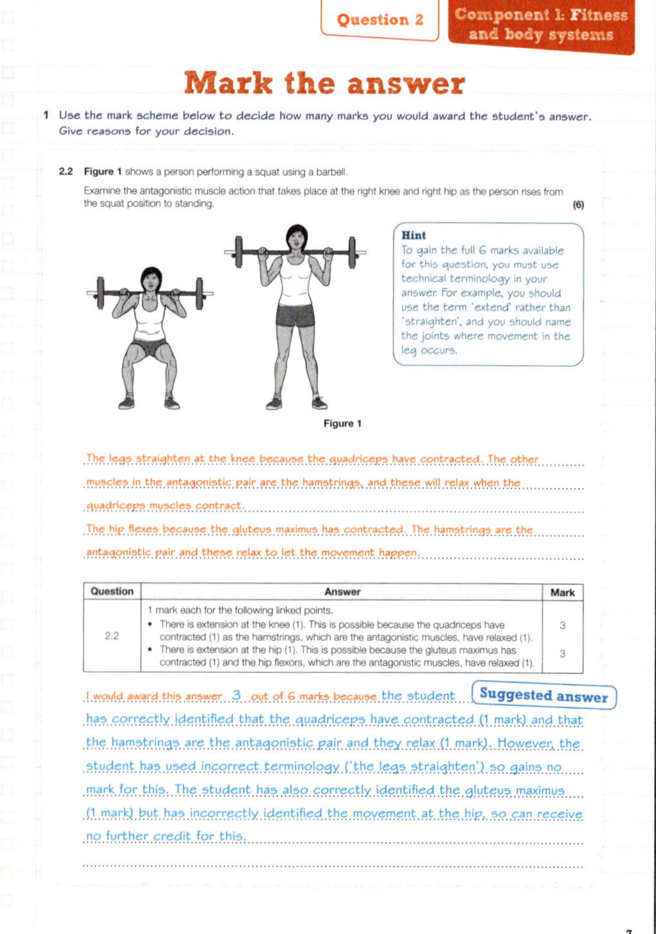

Figure 1

The legs straighten at the knee because the quadriceps have contracted. The other muscles in the antagonistic pair are the hamstrings, and these will relax when the quadriceps muscles contract.

The hip flexes because the gluteus maximus has contracted. The hamstrings are the antagonistic pair and these relax to let the movement happen.

Question	Answer	Mark
2.2	1 mark each for the following linked points. • There is extension at the knee (1). This is possible because the quadriceps have contracted (1) as the hamstrings, which are the antagonistic muscles, have relaxed (1). • There is extension at the hip (1). This is possible because the gluteus maximus has contracted (1) and the hip flexors, which are the antagonistic muscles, have relaxed (1).	3 3

I would award this answer 3 out of 6 marks because the student (Suggested answer) has correctly identified that the quadriceps have contracted (1 mark) and that the hamstrings are the antagonistic pair and they relax (1 mark). However, the student has used incorrect terminology ('the legs straighten') so gains no mark for this. The student has also correctly identified the gluteus maximus (1 mark) but has incorrectly identified the movement at the hip, so can receive no further credit for this.

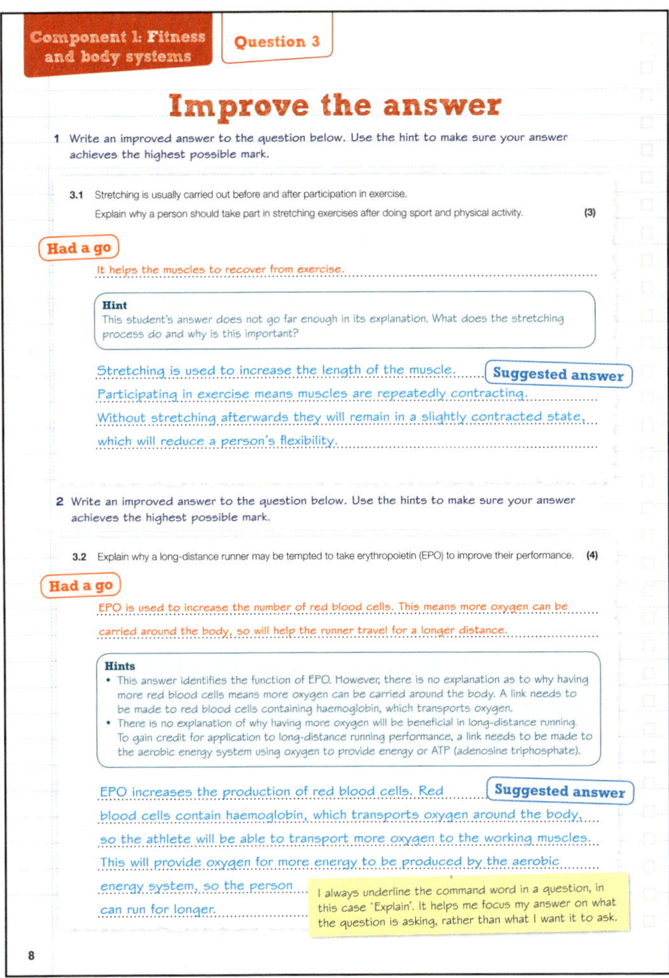

Improve the answer

1 Write an improved answer to the question below. Use the hint to make sure your answer achieves the highest possible mark.

3.1 Stretching is usually carried out before and after participation in exercise.

Explain why a person should take part in stretching exercises after doing sport and physical activity. (3)

Had a go

It helps the muscles to recover from exercise.

Hint
This student's answer does not go far enough in its explanation. What does the stretching process do and why is this important?

Stretching is used to increase the length of the muscle. **Suggested answer**
Participating in exercise means muscles are repeatedly contracting.
Without stretching afterwards they will remain in a slightly contracted state,
which will reduce a person's flexibility.

2 Write an improved answer to the question below. Use the hints to make sure your answer achieves the highest possible mark.

3.2 Explain why a long-distance runner may be tempted to take erythropoietin (EPO) to improve their performance. (4)

Had a go

EPO is used to increase the number of red blood cells. This means more oxygen can be carried around the body, so will help the runner travel for a longer distance.

Hints
- This answer identifies the function of EPO. However, there is no explanation as to why having more red blood cells means more oxygen can be carried around the body. A link needs to be made to red blood cells containing haemoglobin, which transports oxygen.
- There is no explanation of why having more oxygen will be beneficial in long-distance running. To gain credit for application to long-distance running performance, a link needs to be made to the aerobic energy system using oxygen to provide energy or ATP (adenosine triphosphate).

EPO increases the production of red blood cells. Red **Suggested answer**
blood cells contain haemoglobin, which transports oxygen around the body,
so the athlete will be able to transport more oxygen to the working muscles.
This will provide oxygen for more energy to be produced by the aerobic
energy system, so the person
can run for longer.

I always underline the command word in a question, in this case 'Explain'. It helps me focus my answer on what the question is asking, rather than what I want it to ask.

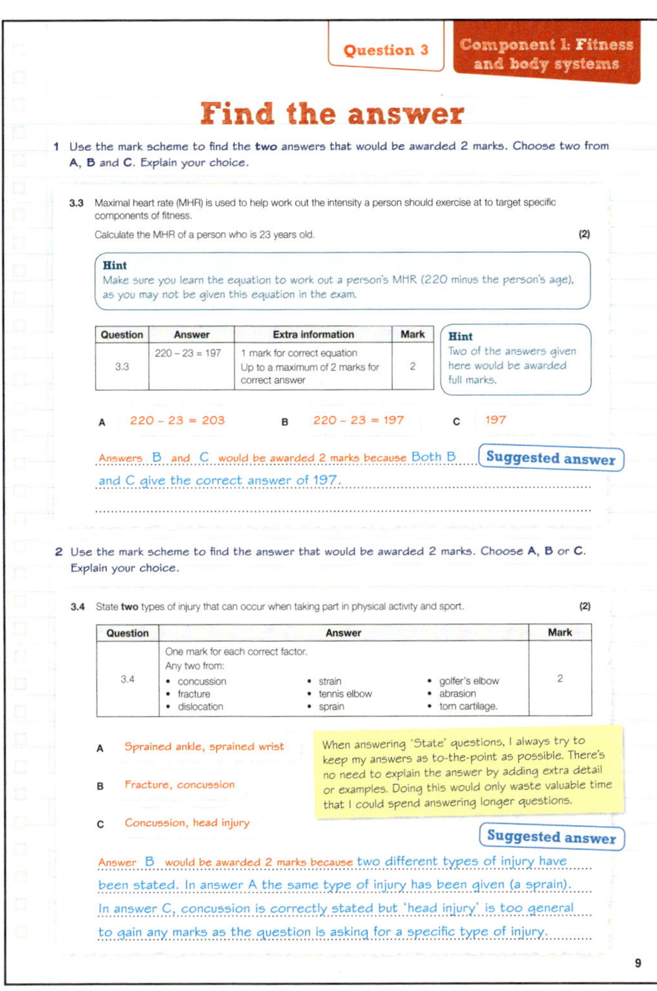

Find the answer

1 Use the mark scheme to find the **two** answers that would be awarded 2 marks. Choose two from A, B and C. Explain your choice.

3.3 Maximal heart rate (MHR) is used to help work out the intensity a person should exercise at to target specific components of fitness.

Calculate the MHR of a person who is 23 years old. (2)

Hint
Make sure you learn the equation to work out a person's MHR (220 minus the person's age), as you may not be given this equation in the exam.

Question	Answer	Extra information	Mark
3.3	220 – 23 = 197	1 mark for correct equation Up to a maximum of 2 marks for correct answer	2

Hint
Two of the answers given here would be awarded full marks.

A 220 – 23 = 203   B 220 – 23 = 197   C 197

Answers B and C would be awarded 2 marks because Both B **Suggested answer**
and C give the correct answer of 197.

2 Use the mark scheme to find the answer that would be awarded 2 marks. Choose A, B or C. Explain your choice.

3.4 State **two** types of injury that can occur when taking part in physical activity and sport. (2)

Question	Answer	Mark
3.4	One mark for each correct factor. Any two from: • concussion • strain • golfer's elbow • fracture • tennis elbow • abrasion • dislocation • sprain • torn cartilage.	2

A Sprained ankle, sprained wrist

B Fracture, concussion

C Concussion, head injury

When answering 'State' questions, I always try to keep my answers as to-the-point as possible. There's no need to explain the answer by adding extra detail or examples. Doing this would only waste valuable time that I could spend answering longer questions.

Suggested answer

Answer B would be awarded 2 marks because two different types of injury have been stated. In answer A the same type of injury has been given (a sprain). In answer C, concussion is correctly stated but 'head injury' is too general to gain any marks as the question is asking for a specific type of injury.

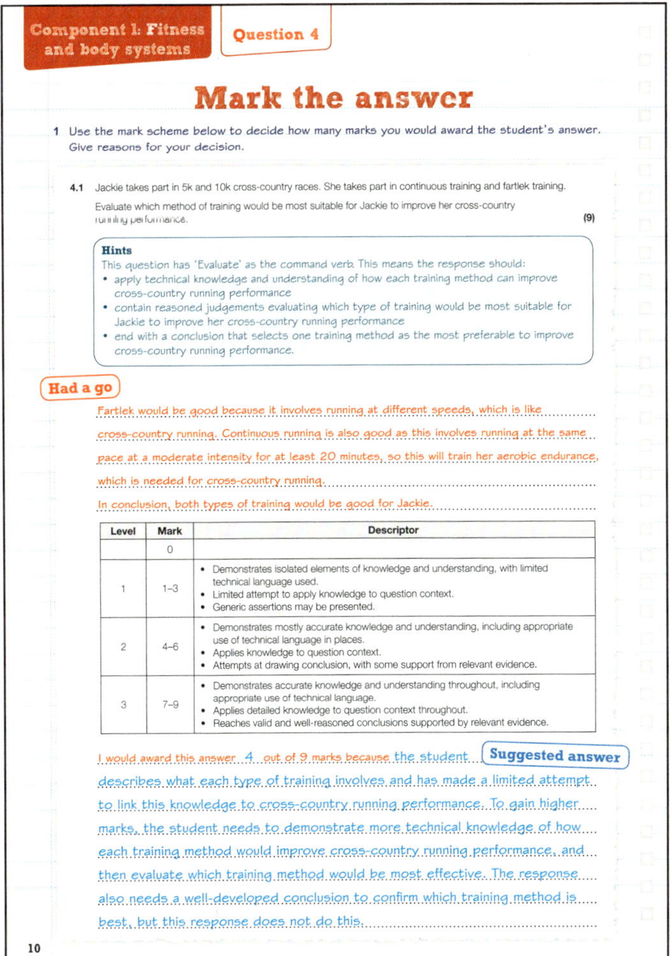

Mark the answer

1 Use the mark scheme below to decide how many marks you would award the student's answer. Give reasons for your decision.

4.1 Jackie takes part in 5k and 10k cross-country races. She takes part in continuous training and fartlek training.

Evaluate which method of training would be most suitable for Jackie to improve her cross-country running performance. (9)

Hints
This question has 'Evaluate' as the command verb. This means the response should:
- apply technical knowledge and understanding of how each training method can improve cross-country running performance
- contain reasoned judgements evaluating which type of training would be most suitable for Jackie to improve her cross-country running performance
- end with a conclusion that selects one training method as the most preferable to improve cross-country running performance.

Had a go

Fartlek would be good because it involves running at different speeds, which is like cross-country running. Continuous running is also good as this involves running at the same pace at a moderate intensity for at least 20 minutes, so this will train her aerobic endurance, which is needed for cross-country running.
In conclusion, both types of training would be good for Jackie.

Level	Mark	Descriptor
	0	
1	1–3	• Demonstrates isolated elements of knowledge and understanding, with limited technical language used. • Limited attempt to apply knowledge to question context. • Generic assertions may be presented.
2	4–6	• Demonstrates mostly accurate knowledge and understanding, including appropriate use of technical language in places. • Applies knowledge to question context. • Attempts at drawing conclusion, with some support from relevant evidence.
3	7–9	• Demonstrates accurate knowledge and understanding throughout, including appropriate use of technical language. • Applies detailed knowledge to question context throughout. • Reaches valid and well-reasoned conclusions supported by relevant evidence.

I would award this answer 4 out of 9 marks because the student **Suggested answer**
describes what each type of training involves and has made a limited attempt
to link this knowledge to cross-country running performance. To gain higher
marks, the student needs to demonstrate more technical knowledge of how
each training method would improve cross-country running performance, and
then evaluate which training method would be most effective. The response
also needs a well-developed conclusion to confirm which training method is
best, but this response does not do this.

Reorder the answer

1 Rearrange the sentences into the most logical order by numbering each part of the student's answer.

4.2 Describe the process of the passage of blood from the body to the heart and then from the heart to the lungs. (4)

Hint
It is important that answers to this type of question are in a logical order. Make sure you read your answer through from the start to check it makes sense.

3 Blood returns to the heart through the pulmonary vein.

1 Blood travels from the body to the heart through the vena cava.

2 Blood travels through the pulmonary artery to the lungs.

4 Blood travels to the body through the aorta.

Suggested answer

2 Rearrange the sentences into the most logical order by numbering each part of the student's answer.

4.3 Explain the process of gaseous exchange in the lungs. (4)

Then I would just need to check the order of the sentences to ensure they are in the correct sequence.

3 There is a higher concentration of carbon dioxide in the blood than in the lungs.

2 Oxygen diffuses from the alveoli into the blood.

1 There is a higher concentration of oxygen in the lungs than in the blood.

4 Carbon dioxide diffuses out of the blood into the alveoli.

Suggested answer

Answers

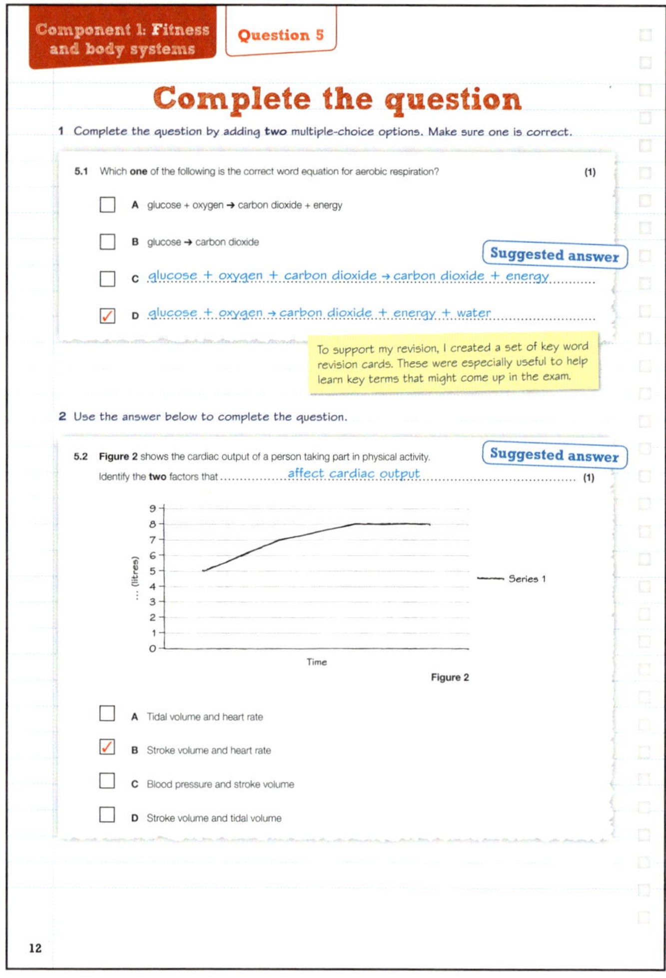

Complete the question

1 Complete the question by adding **two** multiple-choice options. Make sure one is correct.

5.1 Which **one** of the following is the correct word equation for aerobic respiration? (1)

- A   glucose + oxygen → carbon dioxide + energy
- B   glucose → carbon dioxide
- C   glucose + oxygen + carbon dioxide → carbon dioxide + energy *[Suggested answer]*
- ✓ D   glucose + oxygen → carbon dioxide + energy + water *[Suggested answer]*

To support my revision, I created a set of key word revision cards. These were especially useful to help learn key terms that might come up in the exam.

2 Use the answer below to complete the question.

5.2 **Figure 2** shows the cardiac output of a person taking part in physical activity.

Identify the **two** factors that .... affect cardiac output .... (1) *[Suggested answer]*

- A   Tidal volume and heart rate
- ✓ B   Stroke volume and heart rate
- C   Blood pressure and stroke volume
- D   Stroke volume and tidal volume

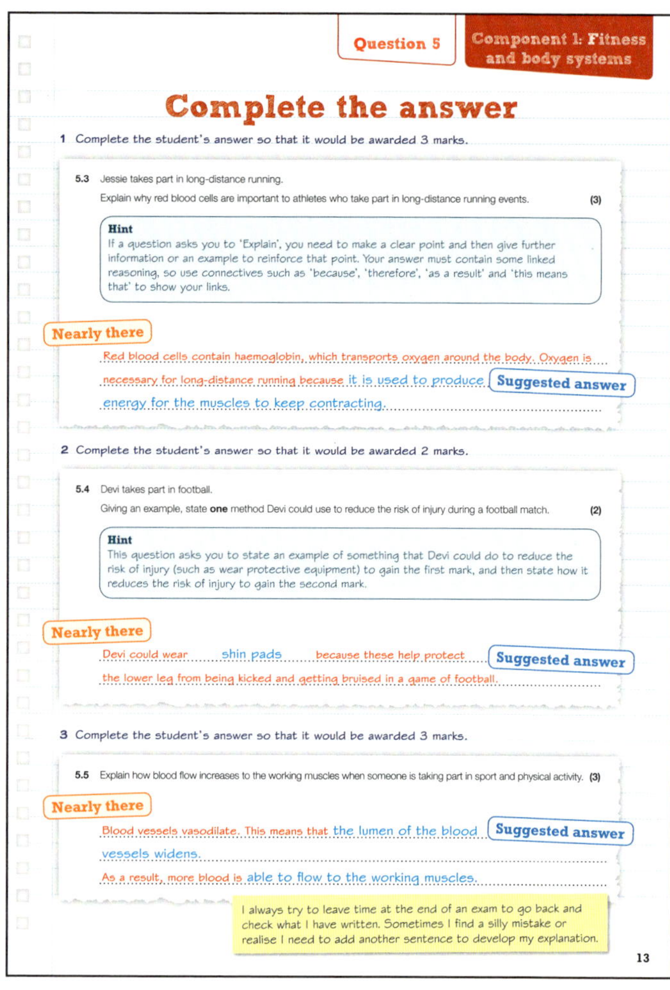

Complete the answer

1 Complete the student's answer so that it would be awarded 3 marks.

5.3 Jessie takes part in long-distance running.

Explain why red blood cells are important to athletes who take part in long-distance running events. (3)

Hint
If a question asks you to 'Explain', you need to make a clear point and then give further information or an example to reinforce that point. Your answer must contain some linked reasoning, so use connectives such as 'because', 'therefore', 'as a result' and 'this means that' to show your links.

Nearly there

Red blood cells contain haemoglobin, which transports oxygen around the body. Oxygen is necessary for long-distance running because it is used to produce energy for the muscles to keep contracting. *[Suggested answer]*

2 Complete the student's answer so that it would be awarded 2 marks.

5.4 Devi takes part in football.

Giving an example, state **one** method Devi could use to reduce the risk of injury during a football match. (2)

Hint
This question asks you to state an example of something that Devi could do to reduce the risk of injury (such as wear protective equipment) to gain the first mark, and then state how it reduces the risk of injury to gain the second mark.

Nearly there

Devi could wear   shin pads   because these help protect the lower leg from being kicked and getting bruised in a game of football. *[Suggested answer]*

3 Complete the student's answer so that it would be awarded 3 marks.

5.5 Explain how blood flow increases to the working muscles when someone is taking part in sport and physical activity. (3)

Nearly there

Blood vessels vasodilate. This means that the lumen of the blood vessels widens. *[Suggested answer]*

As a result, more blood is able to flow to the working muscles.

I always try to leave time at the end of an exam to go back and check what I have written. Sometimes I find a silly mistake or realise I need to add another sentence to develop my explanation.

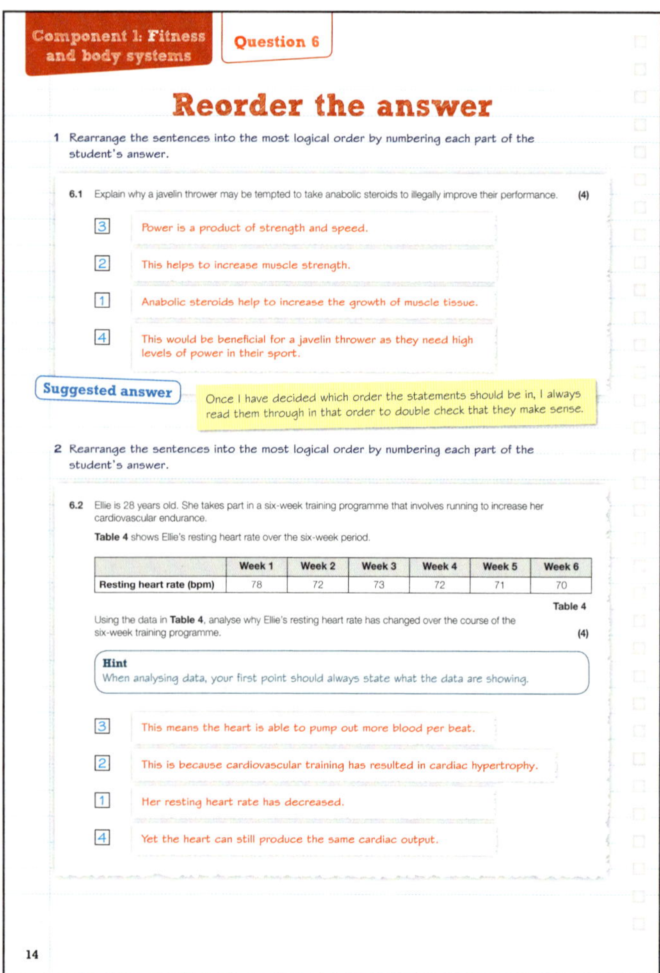

Reorder the answer

1 Rearrange the sentences into the most logical order by numbering each part of the student's answer.

6.1 Explain why a javelin thrower may be tempted to take anabolic steroids to illegally improve their performance. (4)

- [3] Power is a product of strength and speed.
- [2] This helps to increase muscle strength.
- [1] Anabolic steroids help to increase the growth of muscle tissue.
- [4] This would be beneficial for a javelin thrower as they need high levels of power in their sport.

[Suggested answer]

Once I have decided which order the statements should be in, I always read them through in that order to double check that they make sense.

2 Rearrange the sentences into the most logical order by numbering each part of the student's answer.

6.2 Ellie is 28 years old. She takes part in a six-week training programme that involves running to increase her cardiovascular endurance.

Table 4 shows Ellie's resting heart rate over the six-week period.

	Week 1	Week 2	Week 3	Week 4	Week 5	Week 6
Resting heart rate (bpm)	78	72	73	72	71	70

Table 4

Using the data in **Table 4**, analyse why Ellie's resting heart rate has changed over the course of the six-week training programme. (4)

Hint
When analysing data, your first point should always state what the data are showing.

- [3] This means the heart is able to pump out more blood per beat.
- [2] This is because cardiovascular training has resulted in cardiac hypertrophy.
- [1] Her resting heart rate has decreased.
- [4] Yet the heart can still produce the same cardiac output.

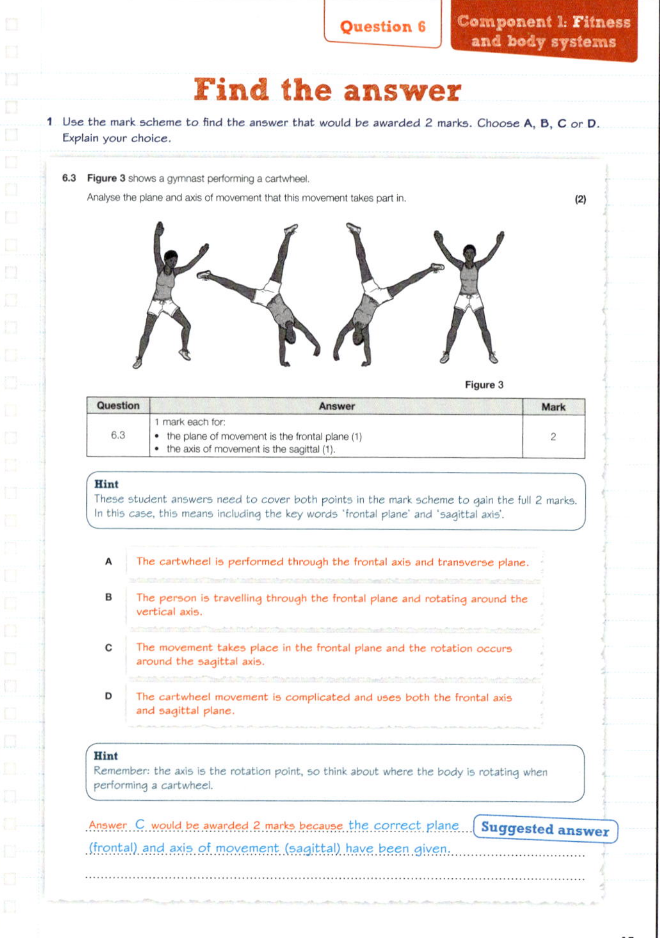

Find the answer

1 Use the mark scheme to find the answer that would be awarded 2 marks. Choose A, B, C or D. Explain your choice.

6.3 **Figure 3** shows a gymnast performing a cartwheel.

Analyse the plane and axis of movement that this movement takes part in. (2)

Figure 3

Question	Answer	Mark
6.3	1 mark each for: • the plane of movement is the frontal plane (1) • the axis of movement is the sagittal (1).	2

Hint
These student answers need to cover both points in the mark scheme to gain the full 2 marks. In this case, this means including the key words 'frontal plane' and 'sagittal axis'.

- A   The cartwheel is performed through the frontal axis and transverse plane.
- B   The person is travelling through the frontal plane and rotating around the vertical axis.
- C   The movement takes place in the frontal plane and the rotation occurs around the sagittal axis.
- D   The cartwheel movement is complicated and uses both the frontal axis and sagittal plane.

Hint
Remember: the axis is the rotation point, so think about where the body is rotating when performing a cartwheel.

Answer C would be awarded 2 marks because the correct plane (frontal) and axis of movement (sagittal) have been given. *[Suggested answer]*

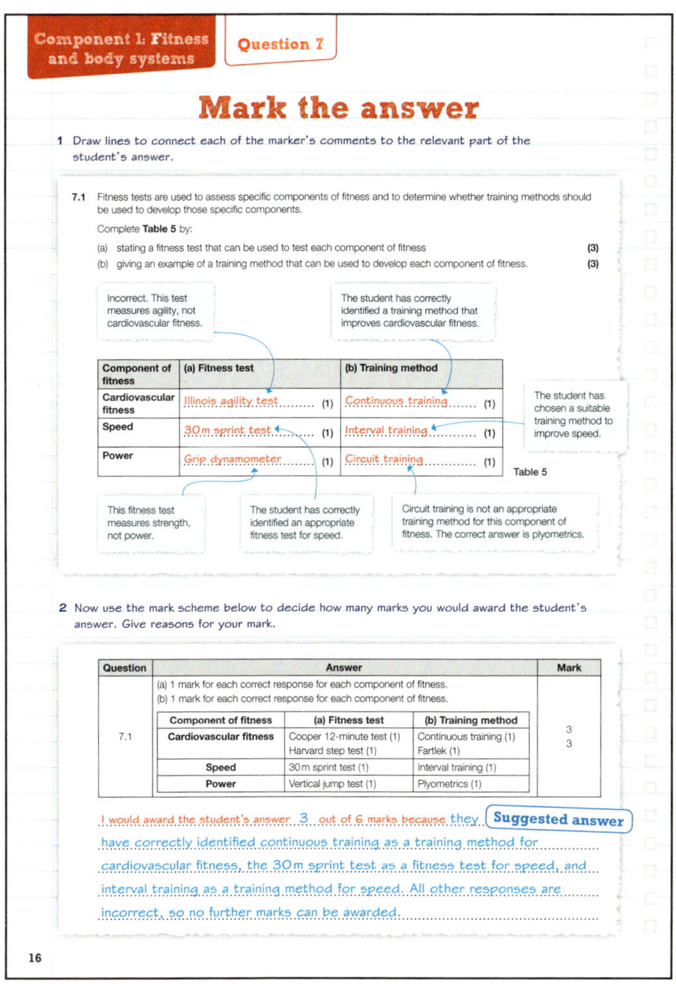

Mark the answer

1 Draw lines to connect each of the marker's comments to the relevant part of the student's answer.

7.1 Fitness tests are used to assess specific components of fitness and to determine whether training methods should be used to develop those specific components.

Complete **Table 5** by:

(a) stating a fitness test that can be used to test each component of fitness   (3)

(b) giving an example of a training method that can be used to develop each component of fitness.   (3)

Incorrect. This test measures agility, not cardiovascular fitness.

The student has correctly identified a training method that improves cardiovascular fitness.

Component of fitness	(a) Fitness test	(b) Training method
Cardiovascular fitness	Illinois agility test (1)	Continuous training (1)
Speed	30 m sprint test (1)	Interval training (1)
Power	Grip dynamometer (1)	Circuit training (1)

Table 5

The student has chosen a suitable training method to improve speed.

This fitness test measures strength, not power.

The student has correctly identified an appropriate fitness test for speed.

Circuit training is not an appropriate training method for this component of fitness. The correct answer is plyometrics.

2 Now use the mark scheme below to decide how many marks you would award the student's answer. Give reasons for your mark.

Question	Answer	Mark
7.1	(a) 1 mark for each correct response for each component of fitness. (b) 1 mark for each correct response for each component of fitness. **Component of fitness / (a) Fitness test / (b) Training method** Cardiovascular fitness — Cooper 12-minute test (1), Harvard step test (1) / Continuous training (1), Fartlek (1) Speed — 30 m sprint test (1) / Interval training (1) Power — Vertical jump test (1) / Plyometrics (1)	3 3

I would award the student's answer **3** out of 6 marks because they [Suggested answer] have correctly identified continuous training as a training method for cardiovascular fitness, the 30 m sprint test as a fitness test for speed, and interval training as a training method for speed. All other responses are incorrect, so no further marks can be awarded.

16

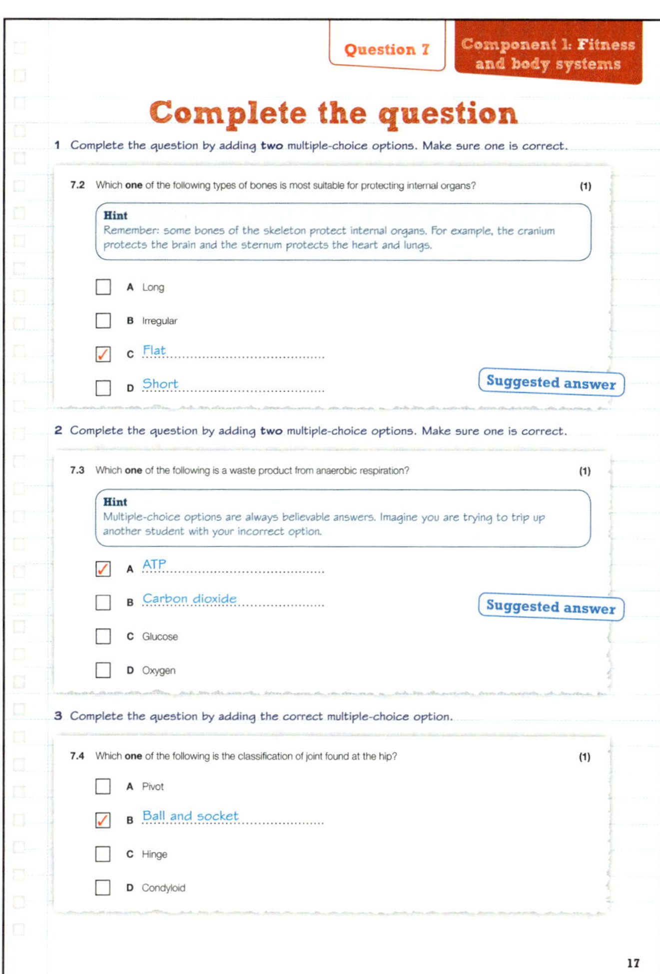

Complete the question

1 Complete the question by adding **two** multiple-choice options. Make sure one is correct.

7.2 Which **one** of the following types of bones is most suitable for protecting internal organs?   (1)

Hint
Remember: some bones of the skeleton protect internal organs. For example, the cranium protects the brain and the sternum protects the heart and lungs.

- [ ] A Long
- [ ] B Irregular
- [x] C Flat
- [ ] D Short

[Suggested answer]

2 Complete the question by adding **two** multiple-choice options. Make sure one is correct.

7.3 Which **one** of the following is a waste product from anaerobic respiration?   (1)

Hint
Multiple-choice options are always believable answers. Imagine you are trying to trip up another student with your incorrect option.

- [x] A ATP
- [ ] B Carbon dioxide
- [ ] C Glucose
- [ ] D Oxygen

[Suggested answer]

3 Complete the question by adding the correct multiple-choice option.

7.4 Which **one** of the following is the classification of joint found at the hip?   (1)

- [ ] A Pivot
- [x] B Ball and socket
- [ ] C Hinge
- [ ] D Condyloid

17

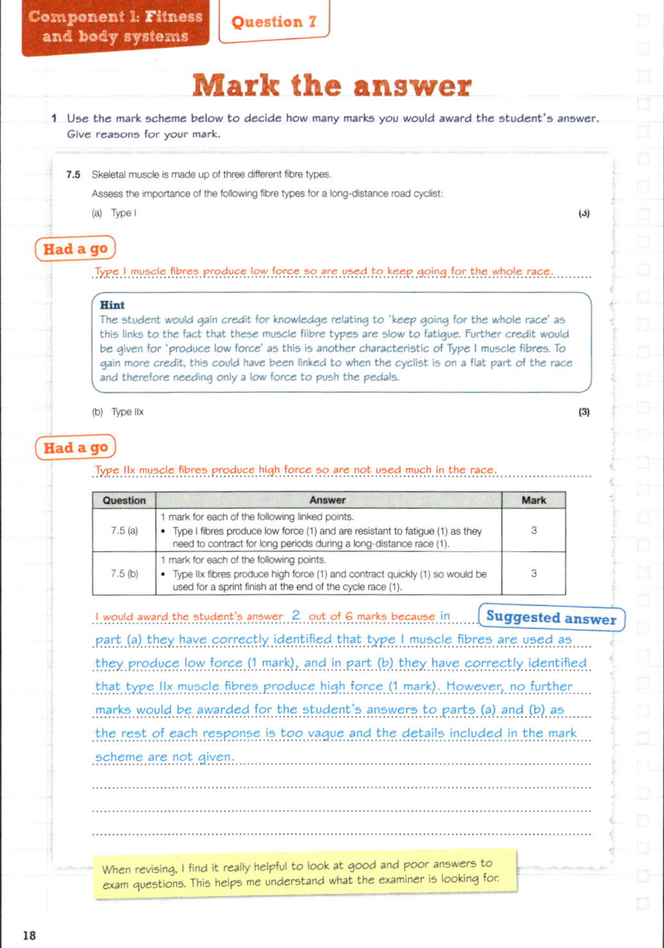

Mark the answer

1 Use the mark scheme below to decide how many marks you would award the student's answer. Give reasons for your mark.

7.5 Skeletal muscle is made up of three different fibre types.

Assess the importance of the following fibre types for a long-distance road cyclist:

(a) Type I   (3)

Had a go

Type I muscle fibres produce low force so are used to keep going for the whole race.

Hint
The student would gain credit for knowledge relating to 'keep going for the whole race' as this links to the fact that these muscle fibre types are slow to fatigue. Further credit would be given for 'produce low force' as this is another characteristic of Type I muscle fibres. To gain more credit, this could have been linked to when the cyclist is on a flat part of the race and therefore needing only a low force to push the pedals.

(b) Type IIx   (3)

Had a go

Type IIx muscle fibres produce high force so are not used much in the race.

Question	Answer	Mark
7.5 (a)	1 mark for each of the following linked points. • Type I fibres produce low force (1) and are resistant to fatigue (1) as they need to contract for long periods during a long-distance race (1).	3
7.5 (b)	1 mark for each of the following points. • Type IIx fibres produce high force (1) and contract quickly (1) so would be used for a sprint finish at the end of the cycle race (1).	3

I would award the student's answer **2** out of 6 marks because in [Suggested answer] part (a) they have correctly identified that type I muscle fibres are used as they produce low force (1 mark), and in part (b) they have correctly identified that type IIx muscle fibres produce high force (1 mark). However, no further marks would be awarded for the student's answers to parts (a) and (b) as the rest of each response is too vague and the details included in the mark scheme are not given.

When revising, I find it really helpful to look at good and poor answers to exam questions. This helps me understand what the examiner is looking for.

18

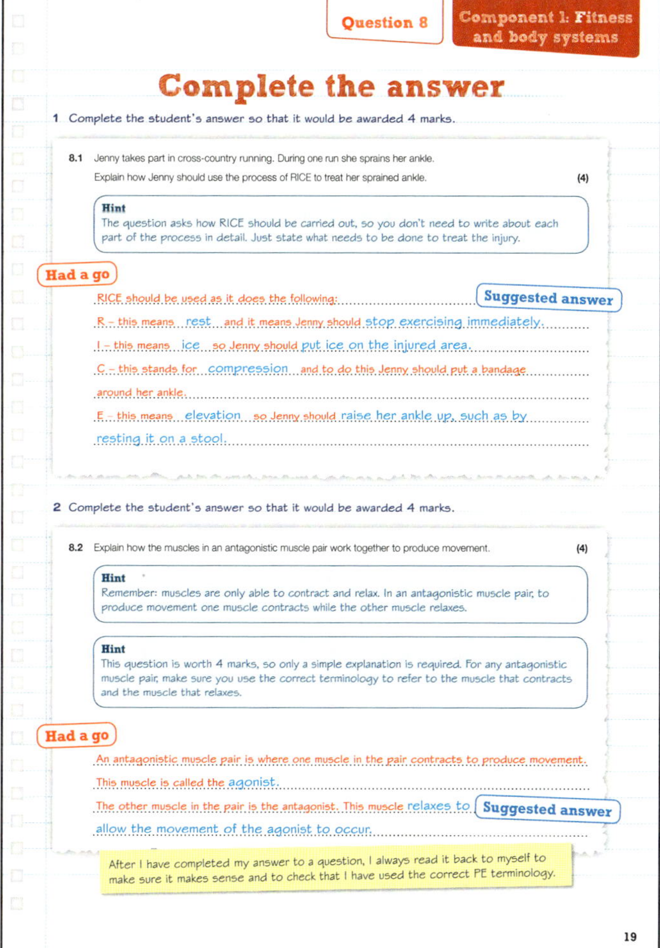

Complete the answer

1 Complete the student's answer so that it would be awarded 4 marks.

8.1 Jenny takes part in cross-country running. During one run she sprains her ankle.

Explain how Jenny should use the process of RICE to treat her sprained ankle.   (4)

Hint
The question asks how RICE should be carried out, so you don't need to write about each part of the process in detail. Just state what needs to be done to treat the injury.

Had a go

RICE should be used as it does the following: [Suggested answer]

R – this means **rest** and it means Jenny should stop exercising immediately.

I – this means **ice** so Jenny should put ice on the injured area.

C – this stands for **compression** and to do this Jenny should put a bandage around her ankle.

E – this means **elevation** so Jenny should raise her ankle up, such as by resting it on a stool.

2 Complete the student's answer so that it would be awarded 4 marks.

8.2 Explain how the muscles in an antagonistic muscle pair work together to produce movement.   (4)

Hint
Remember: muscles are only able to contract and relax. In an antagonistic muscle pair, to produce movement one muscle contracts while the other muscle relaxes.

Hint
This question is worth 4 marks, so only a simple explanation is required. For any antagonistic muscle pair, make sure you use the correct terminology to refer to the muscle that contracts and the muscle that relaxes.

Had a go

An antagonistic muscle pair is where one muscle in the pair contracts to produce movement. This muscle is called the agonist.

The other muscle in the pair is the antagonist. This muscle relaxes to [Suggested answer] allow the movement of the agonist to occur.

After I have completed my answer to a question, I always read it back to myself to make sure it makes sense and to check that I have used the correct PE terminology.

19

Complete the question

1 Use the hints and the student's answers below to complete questions 8.3 (a) and 8.3 (b).

8.3 **Figure 4** shows a person's heart rate at rest and during exercise.

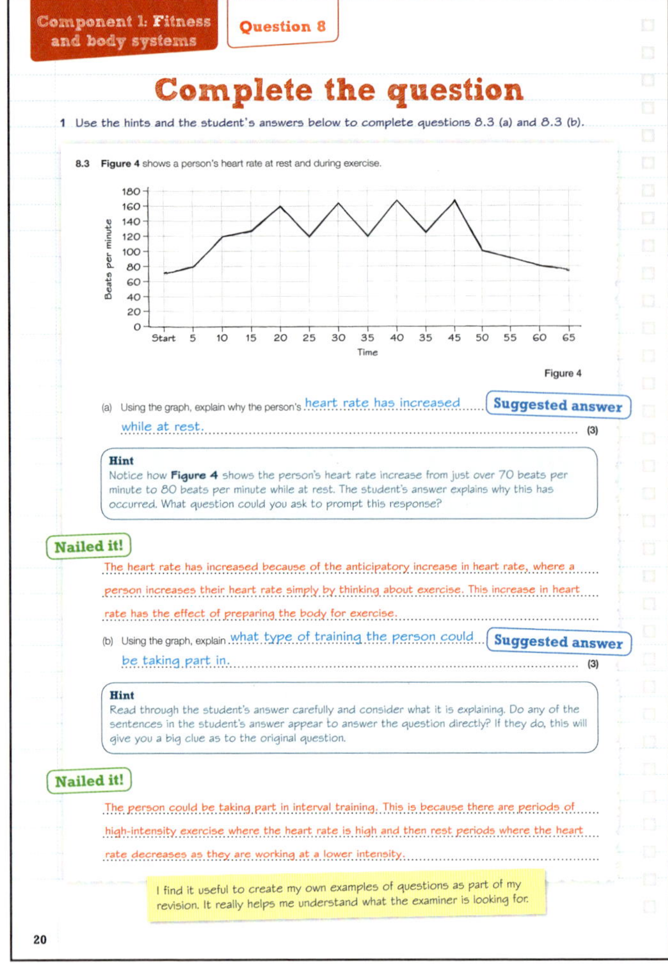

Figure 4

(a) Using the graph, explain why the person's <u>heart rate has increased while at rest.</u> **Suggested answer** (3)

Hint
Notice how **Figure 4** shows the person's heart rate increase from just over 70 beats per minute to 80 beats per minute while at rest. The student's answer explains why this has occurred. What question could you ask to prompt this response?

Nailed it!

The heart rate has increased because of the anticipatory increase in heart rate, where a person increases their heart rate simply by thinking about exercise. This increase in heart rate has the effect of preparing the body for exercise.

(b) Using the graph, explain <u>what type of training the person could be taking part in.</u> **Suggested answer** (3)

Hint
Read through the student's answer carefully and consider what it is explaining. Do any of the sentences in the student's answer appear to answer the question directly? If they do, this will give you a big clue as to the original question.

Nailed it!

The person could be taking part in interval training. This is because there are periods of high-intensity exercise where the heart rate is high and then rest periods where the heart rate decreases as they are working at a lower intensity.

> I find it useful to create my own examples of questions as part of my revision. It really helps me understand what the examiner is looking for.

Find the answer

1 Use the mark scheme to find the student answer that would be awarded full marks. Choose **A**, **B**, **C** or **D**.

8.4 **Figure 5** shows a lever system.

Identify the parts of the lever system. (3)

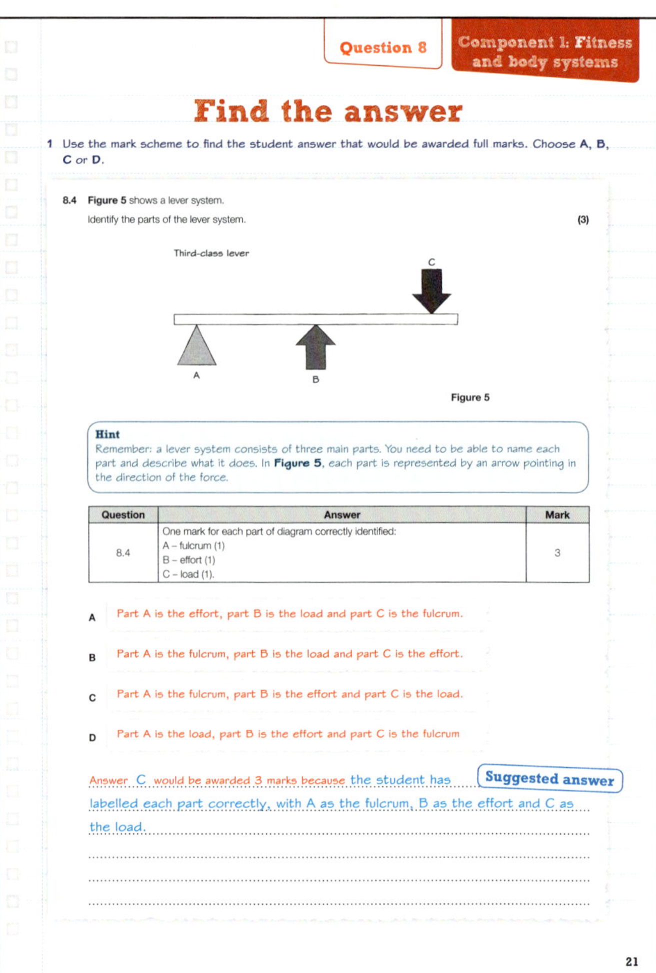

Hint
Remember: a lever system consists of three main parts. You need to be able to name each part and describe what it does. In **Figure 5**, each part is represented by an arrow pointing in the direction of the force.

Question	Answer	Mark
8.4	One mark for each part of diagram correctly identified: A – fulcrum (1) B – effort (1) C – load (1).	3

A   Part A is the effort, part B is the load and part C is the fulcrum.

B   Part A is the fulcrum, part B is the load and part C is the effort.

C   Part A is the fulcrum, part B is the effort and part C is the load.

D   Part A is the load, part B is the effort and part C is the fulcrum

Suggested answer

Answer C would be awarded 3 marks because the student has labelled each part correctly, with A as the fulcrum, B as the effort and C as the load.

Find the answer

1 Use the mark scheme to find the student answer that would be awarded full marks. Choose **A**, **B**, **C** or **D**.

9.1 Describe a third-class lever system found in the body. (4)

Hint
Remember: the location of each part of the lever system determines which type of lever it is.

> I always use the mnemonic 'FLE' to help me remember which lever system is which.
> - First-class lever systems have the **F**ulcrum in the middle.
> - Second-class lever systems have the **L**oad in the middle.
> - Third-class lever systems have the **E**ffort in the middle.

Question	Answer	Mark
9.1	Award marks for: • location in body (1) • identification of effort in body (1) • identification of fulcrum in body (1) • identification of load in body (1). For example: • At the arm (1), with the biceps producing effort (1), the elbow acting as the fulcrum (1), and the hand and lower arm acting as the load (1).	4

A   This type of lever can be found in the arm, with the elbow as the fulcrum and the weight of the hand as the load.

B   The arm has this type of lever, with the biceps producing the effort, the elbow acting as the fulcrum, and the lower arm and hand (and anything the hand is holding) acting as the load.

C   The arm is a third-class lever. The elbow acts as the fulcrum, the triceps produce the effort, and the hand is the load.

D   A third-class lever can be found in the arm, with the fulcrum at the elbow.

Suggested answer

Answer B would be awarded 4 marks because the student has correctly located a third-class lever system in the body (the arm), and correctly identified what functions as the effort (the biceps), the fulcrum (the elbow) and the load (the hand).

> I really struggled with understanding where the three types of lever system are found in the body, so I learned specific examples of each type and the bones, muscles and joints involved. I even practised moving my body while calling out the different names and their role in the lever system – this made the theory so much easier to understand!

Mark the answer

1 Use the mark scheme below to decide how many marks you would award the student's answer. Give reasons for your mark.

9.2 **Figure 6** is a diagram of the skeletal system.

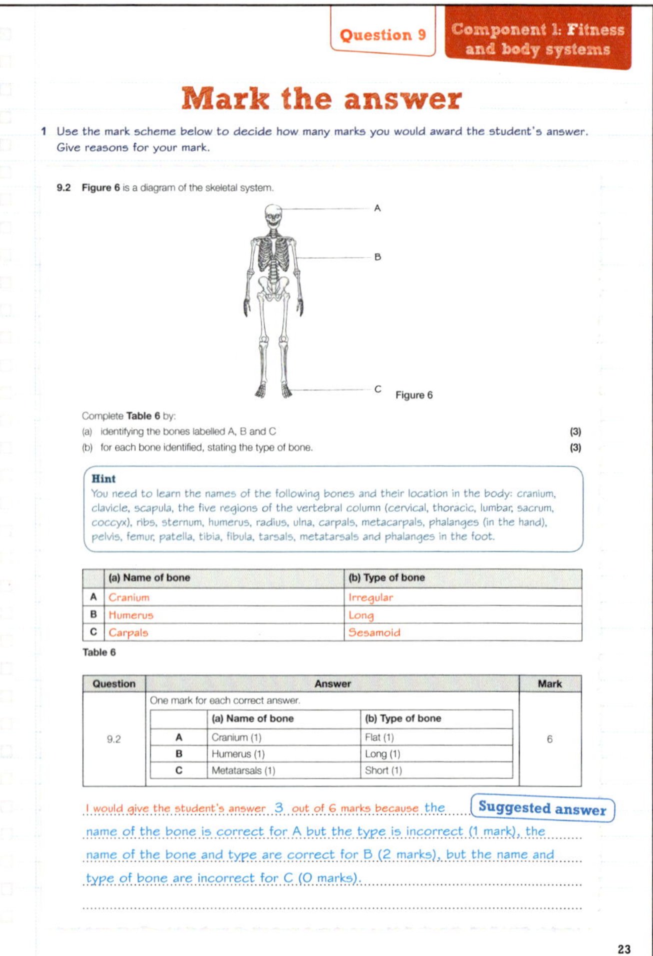

Complete **Table 6** by:
(a) identifying the bones labelled A, B and C (3)
(b) for each bone identified, stating the type of bone. (3)

Hint
You need to learn the names of the following bones and their location in the body: cranium, clavicle, scapula, the five regions of the vertebral column (cervical, thoracic, lumbar, sacrum, coccyx), ribs, sternum, humerus, radius, ulna, carpals, metacarpals, phalanges (in the hand), pelvis, femur, patella, tibia, fibula, tarsals, metatarsals and phalanges in the foot.

	(a) Name of bone	(b) Type of bone
A	Cranium	Irregular
B	Humerus	Long
C	Carpals	Sesamoid

Table 6

Question	Answer			Mark
9.2	One mark for each correct answer.			6
		(a) Name of bone	(b) Type of bone	
	A	Cranium (1)	Flat (1)	
	B	Humerus (1)	Long (1)	
	C	Metatarsals (1)	Short (1)	

Suggested answer

I would give the student's answer 3 out of 6 marks because the name of the bone is correct for A but the type is incorrect (1 mark), the name of the bone and type are correct for B (2 marks), but the name and type of bone are incorrect for C (0 marks).

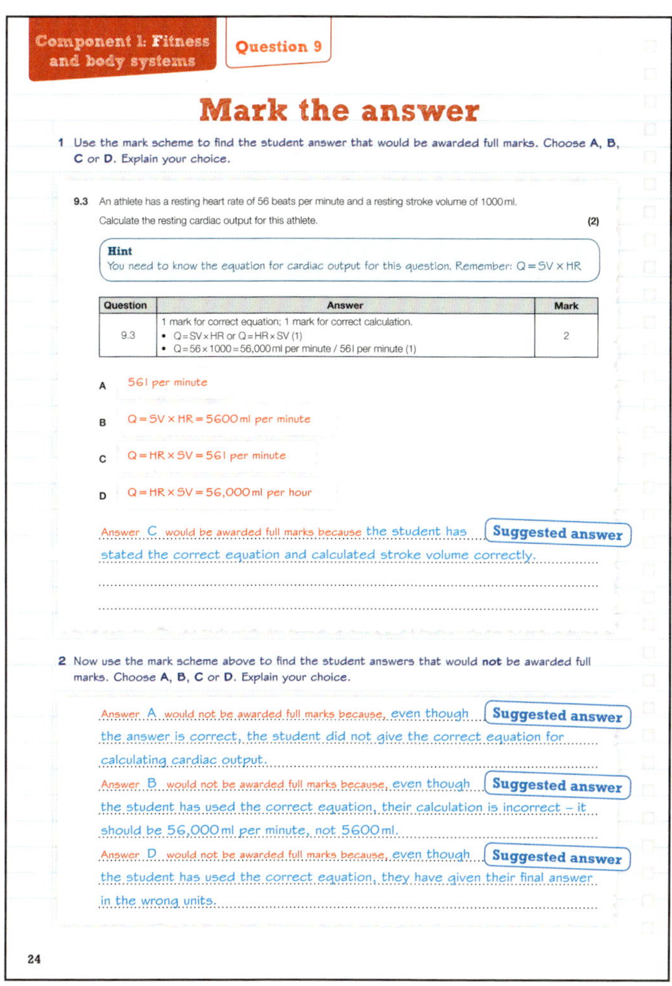

Mark the answer

1 Use the mark scheme to find the student answer that would be awarded full marks. Choose A, B, C or D. Explain your choice.

9.3 An athlete has a resting heart rate of 56 beats per minute and a resting stroke volume of 1000 ml.
Calculate the resting cardiac output for this athlete. (2)

Hint
You need to know the equation for cardiac output for this question. Remember: $Q = SV \times HR$

Question	Answer	Mark
9.3	1 mark for correct equation; 1 mark for correct calculation. • $Q = SV \times HR$ or $Q = HR \times SV$ (1) • $Q = 56 \times 1000 = 56{,}000$ ml per minute / 56 l per minute (1)	2

A 56 l per minute

B $Q = SV \times HR = 5600$ ml per minute

C $Q = HR \times SV = 56$ l per minute

D $Q = HR \times SV = 56{,}000$ ml per hour

Answer C would be awarded full marks because [Suggested answer] the student has stated the correct equation and calculated stroke volume correctly.

2 Now use the mark scheme above to find the student answers that would **not** be awarded full marks. Choose A, B, C or D. Explain your choice.

Answer A would not be awarded full marks because, even though [Suggested answer] the answer is correct, the student did not give the correct equation for calculating cardiac output.

Answer B would not be awarded full marks because, even though [Suggested answer] the student has used the correct equation, their calculation is incorrect – it should be 56,000 ml per minute, not 5600 ml.

Answer D would not be awarded full marks because, even though [Suggested answer] the student has used the correct equation, they have given their final answer in the wrong units.

24

Complete the answer

1 Use the hints below to complete the student's answers so that parts (a) and (b) would each be awarded 3 marks.

10.1 Vasilis takes part in a cycle race. The race involves cycling 75 miles, mainly on flat roads but with some steep hills.
(a) Explain the type of muscle fibres used by Vasilis on flat roads during the cycle race. (3)

Hint
The race is a long distance one, so it is important that the muscle fibres do not fatigue. You need to complete the student's answer by explaining why Type I muscle fibres would mostly be used during the flat parts of the race.

Had a go
Vasilis would use type I muscle fibres on the flat roads because these [Suggested answer] muscles are able to continually contract and are slow to fatigue, allowing Vasilis to cycle the full distance of the race.

(b) Explain the type of muscle fibres used by Vasilis to climb steep hills during the cycle race. (3)

Hint
There are two types of fast-twitch muscle fibre. The type that produces the highest force would be most appropriate for cycling up a hill. You need to complete the student's answer by explaining why.

Had a go
Vasilis would use type IIx muscle fibres for cycling up hills because [Suggested answer] these produce contractions with high force to push the pedals hard enough to get up the hill at speed.

2 Complete the student's answer so that it would be awarded 4 marks.

10.2 Explain **two** characteristics of type IIx muscle fibres. (4)

Nearly there
Characteristic 1: Type IIx muscle fibres fatigue quickly as they do not have [Suggested answer] enough mitochondria to produce energy through the aerobic energy system.

Nearly there
Characteristic 2: Type IIx muscle fibres can contract quickly, which means [Suggested answer] they can generate high levels of power.

I find it really helpful to underline the key words in a question, especially when the question is long. It helps me focus on what I have to do.

25

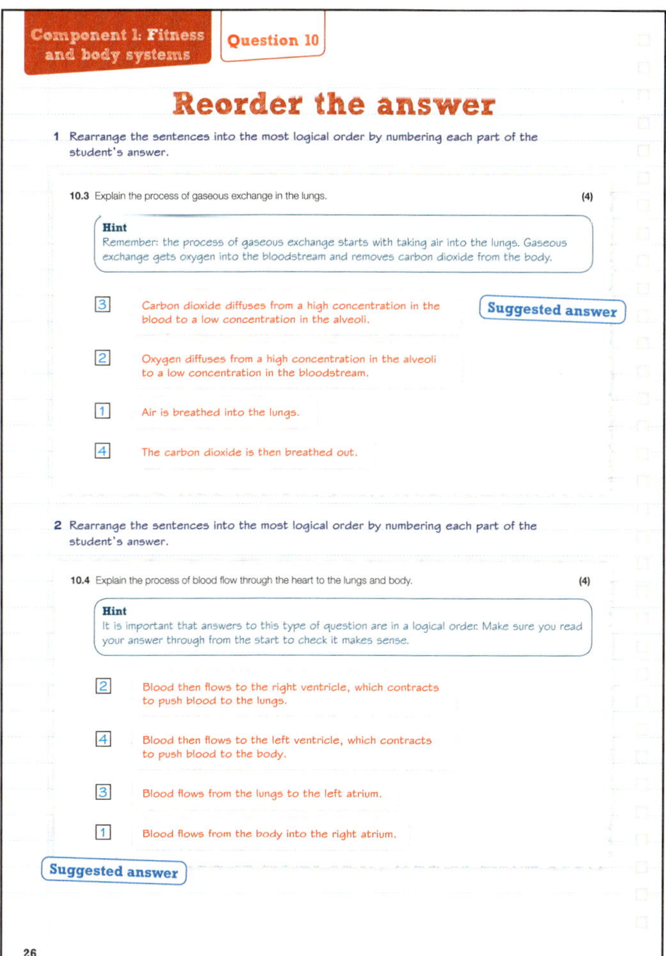

Reorder the answer

1 Rearrange the sentences into the most logical order by numbering each part of the student's answer.

10.3 Explain the process of gaseous exchange in the lungs. (4)

Hint
Remember: the process of gaseous exchange starts with taking air into the lungs. Gaseous exchange gets oxygen into the bloodstream and removes carbon dioxide from the body.

[3] Carbon dioxide diffuses from a high concentration in the blood to a low concentration in the alveoli. [Suggested answer]

[2] Oxygen diffuses from a high concentration in the alveoli to a low concentration in the bloodstream.

[1] Air is breathed into the lungs.

[4] The carbon dioxide is then breathed out.

2 Rearrange the sentences into the most logical order by numbering each part of the student's answer.

10.4 Explain the process of blood flow through the heart to the lungs and body. (4)

Hint
It is important that answers to this type of question are in a logical order. Make sure you read your answer through from the start to check it makes sense.

[2] Blood then flows to the right ventricle, which contracts to push blood to the lungs.

[4] Blood then flows to the left ventricle, which contracts to push blood to the body.

[3] Blood flows from the lungs to the left atrium.

[1] Blood flows from the body into the right atrium.

[Suggested answer]

26

Improve the answer

1 Use the hint below to write an improved student answer that would be awarded 2 marks.

10.5 Blood is made up of red and white blood cells, platelets and plasma.
(a) Describe the function of red blood cells. (2)

Had a go
The function of red blood cells is to carry oxygen around the body.

Hint
To gain the full 2 marks for a 'Describe' question, you need to identify what has been asked for (the 'function of red blood cells') then describe how this is done by giving further details. This student's answer would only gain the first mark. Improve the answer so it would be awarded full marks.

The function of red blood cells is to carry oxygen around [Suggested answer] the body. They can do this because they contain haemoglobin, which binds to oxygen.

2 Use the hint below to write an improved student answer that would be awarded 2 marks.

(b) Describe the function of white blood cells. (2)

Had a go
White blood cells fight infection.

Hint
As the question is worth 2 marks, you will need to make two distinct points to be awarded full marks. This student's answer only makes one distinct point. To improve the answer, you need to go on to describe how white blood cells do this.

White blood cells fight infection by destroying germs to [Suggested answer] prevent us from becoming ill.

I always underline the command word in a question ('Describe', in this instance). It helps me focus my answer on what the question is asking rather than what I want it to ask.

27

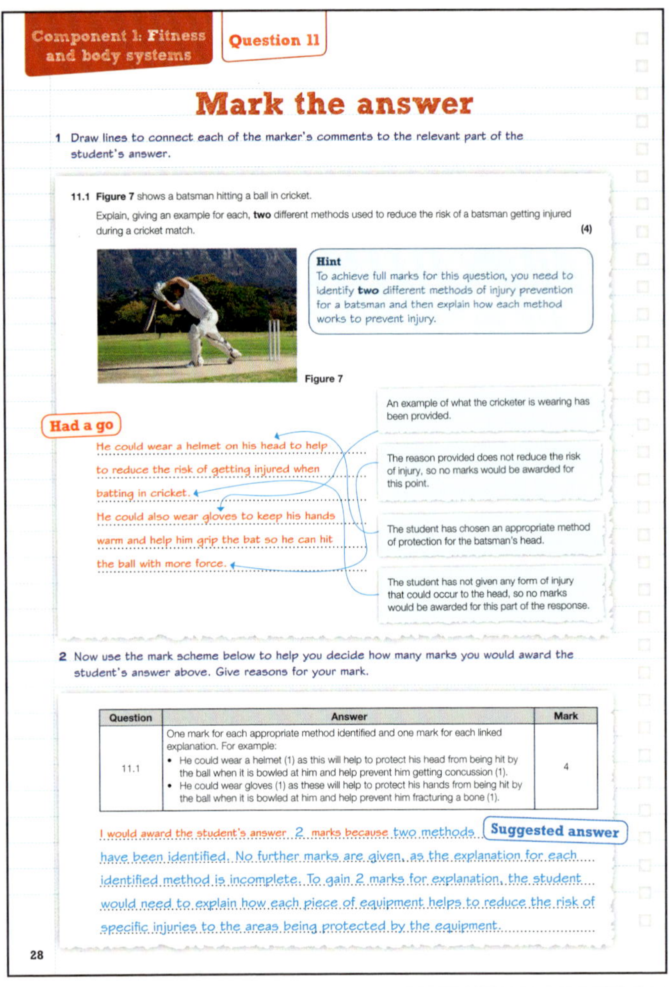

Mark the answer

1 Draw lines to connect each of the marker's comments to the relevant part of the student's answer.

11.1 **Figure 7** shows a batsman hitting a ball in cricket.

Explain, giving an example for each, **two** different methods used to reduce the risk of a batsman getting injured during a cricket match. (4)

Hint
To achieve full marks for this question, you need to identify **two** different methods of injury prevention for a batsman and then explain how each method works to prevent injury.

Figure 7

Had a go

He could wear a helmet on his head to help to reduce the risk of getting injured when batting in cricket.

He could also wear gloves to keep his hands warm and help him grip the bat so he can hit the ball with more force.

Marker's comments:
- An example of what the cricketer is wearing has been provided.
- The reason provided does not reduce the risk of injury, so no marks would be awarded for this point.
- The student has chosen an appropriate method of protection for the batsman's head.
- The student has not given any form of injury that could occur to the head, so no marks would be awarded for this part of the response.

2 Now use the mark scheme below to help you decide how many marks you would award the student's answer above. Give reasons for your mark.

Question	Answer	Mark
11.1	One mark for each appropriate method identified and one mark for each linked explanation. For example: • He could wear a helmet (1) as this will help to protect his head from being hit by the ball when it is bowled at him and help prevent him getting concussion (1). • He could wear gloves (1) as these will help to protect his hands from being hit by the ball when it is bowled at him and help prevent him fracturing a bone (1).	4

Suggested answer

I would award the student's answer 2 marks because two methods have been identified. No further marks are given, as the explanation for each identified method is incomplete. To gain 2 marks for explanation, the student would need to explain how each piece of equipment helps to reduce the risk of specific injuries to the areas being protected by the equipment.

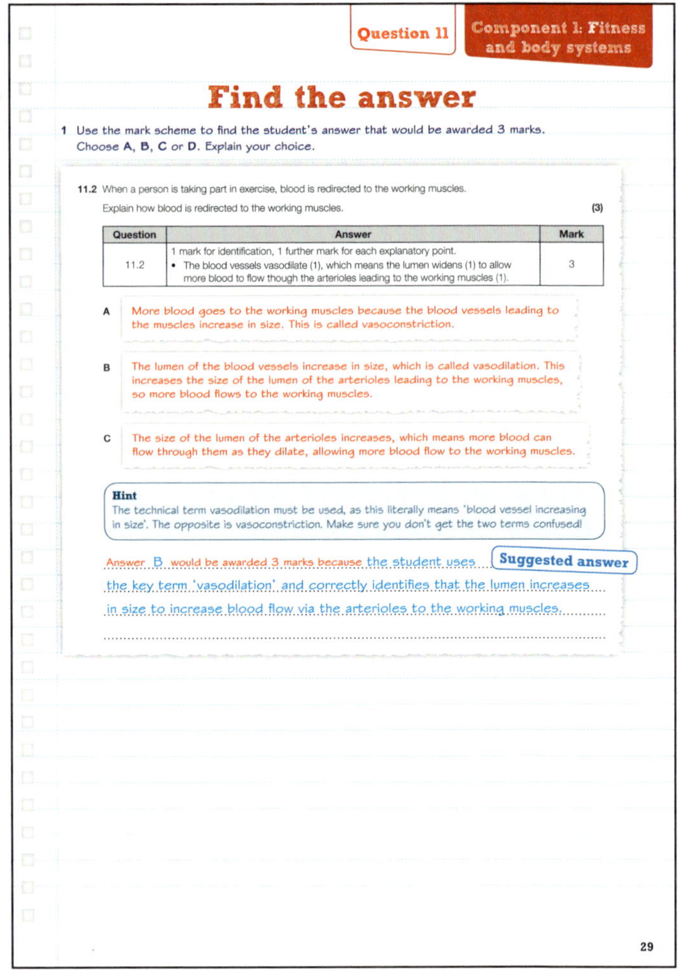

Find the answer

1 Use the mark scheme to find the student's answer that would be awarded 3 marks. Choose A, B, C or D. Explain your choice.

11.2 When a person is taking part in exercise, blood is redirected to the working muscles.

Explain how blood is redirected to the working muscles. (3)

Question	Answer	Mark
11.2	1 mark for identification, 1 further mark for each explanatory point. • The blood vessels vasodilate (1), which means the lumen widens (1) to allow more blood to flow though the arterioles leading to the working muscles (1).	3

A More blood goes to the working muscles because the blood vessels leading to the muscles increase in size. This is called vasoconstriction.

B The lumen of the blood vessels increase in size, which is called vasodilation. This increases the size of the lumen of the arterioles leading to the working muscles, so more blood flows to the working muscles.

C The size of the lumen of the arterioles increases, which means more blood can flow through them as they dilate, allowing more blood flow to the working muscles.

Hint
The technical term vasodilation must be used, as this literally means 'blood vessel increasing in size'. The opposite is vasoconstriction. Make sure you don't get the two terms confused!

Suggested answer

Answer B would be awarded 3 marks because the student uses the key term 'vasodilation' and correctly identifies that the lumen increases in size to increase blood flow via the arterioles to the working muscles.

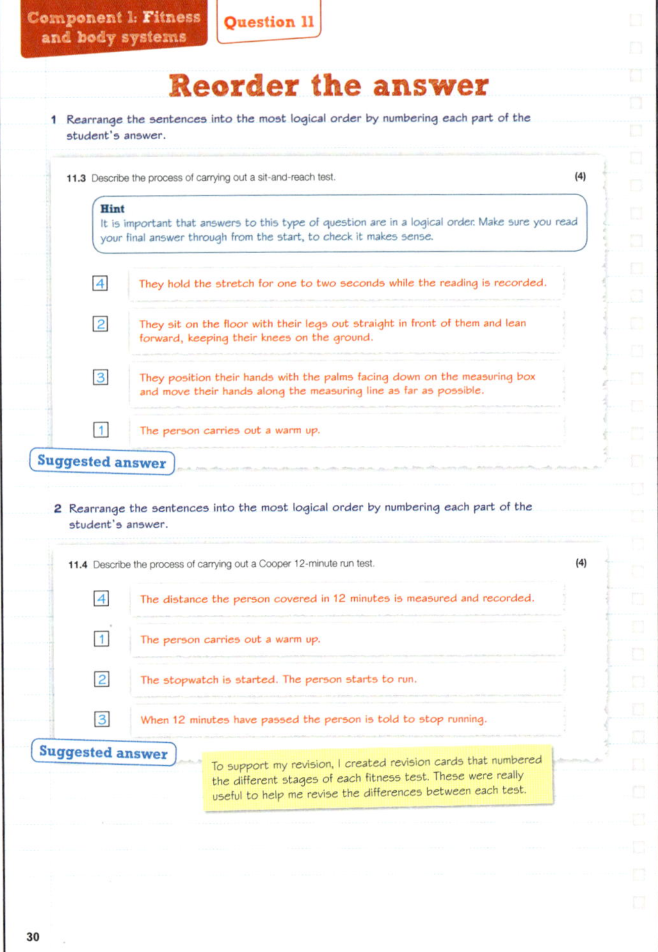

Reorder the answer

1 Rearrange the sentences into the most logical order by numbering each part of the student's answer.

11.3 Describe the process of carrying out a sit-and-reach test. (4)

Hint
It is important that answers to this type of question are in a logical order. Make sure you read your final answer through from the start, to check it makes sense.

- [4] They hold the stretch for one to two seconds while the reading is recorded.
- [2] They sit on the floor with their legs out straight in front of them and lean forward, keeping their knees on the ground.
- [3] They position their hands with the palms facing down on the measuring box and move their hands along the measuring line as far as possible.
- [1] The person carries out a warm up.

Suggested answer

2 Rearrange the sentences into the most logical order by numbering each part of the student's answer.

11.4 Describe the process of carrying out a Cooper 12-minute run test. (4)

- [4] The distance the person covered in 12 minutes is measured and recorded.
- [1] The person carries out a warm up.
- [2] The stopwatch is started. The person starts to run.
- [3] When 12 minutes have passed the person is told to stop running.

Suggested answer

> To support my revision, I created revision cards that numbered the different stages of each fitness test. These were really useful to help me revise the differences between each test.

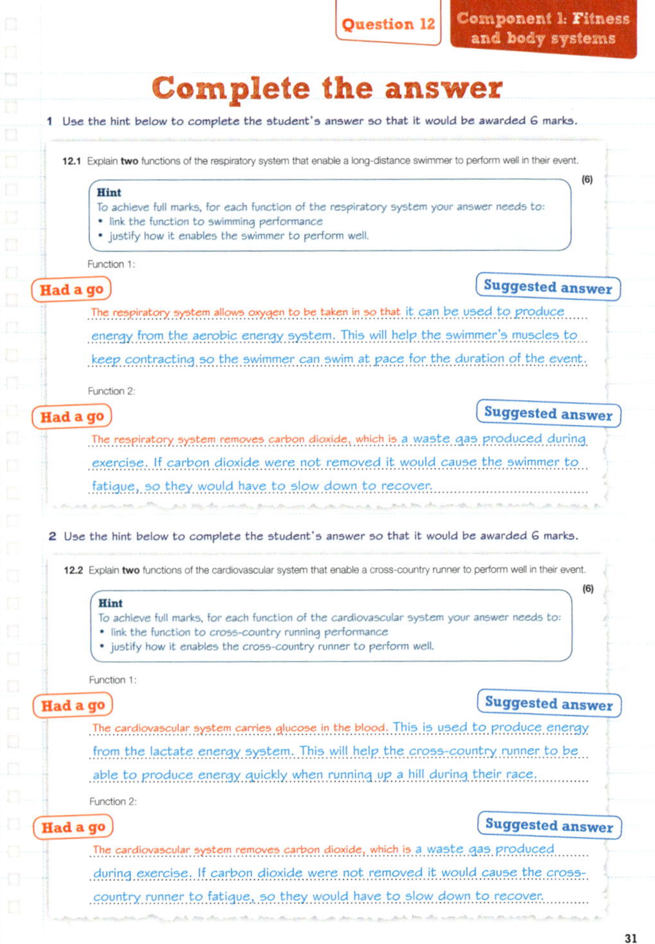

Complete the answer

1 Use the hint below to complete the student's answer so that it would be awarded 6 marks.

12.1 Explain **two** functions of the respiratory system that enable a long-distance swimmer to perform well in their event. (6)

Hint
To achieve full marks, for each function of the respiratory system your answer needs to:
- link the function to swimming performance
- justify how it enables the swimmer to perform well.

Function 1:

Had a go / **Suggested answer**

The respiratory system allows oxygen to be taken in so that it can be used to produce energy from the aerobic energy system. This will help the swimmer's muscles to keep contracting so the swimmer can swim at pace for the duration of the event.

Function 2:

Had a go / **Suggested answer**

The respiratory system removes carbon dioxide, which is a waste gas produced during exercise. If carbon dioxide were not removed it would cause the swimmer to fatigue, so they would have to slow down to recover.

2 Use the hint below to complete the student's answer so that it would be awarded 6 marks.

12.2 Explain **two** functions of the cardiovascular system that enable a cross-country runner to perform well in their event. (6)

Hint
To achieve full marks, for each function of the cardiovascular system your answer needs to:
- link the function to cross-country running performance
- justify how it enables the cross-country runner to perform well.

Function 1:

Had a go / **Suggested answer**

The cardiovascular system carries glucose in the blood. This is used to produce energy from the lactate energy system. This will help the cross-country runner to be able to produce energy quickly when running up a hill during their race.

Function 2:

Had a go / **Suggested answer**

The cardiovascular system removes carbon dioxide, which is a waste gas produced during exercise. If carbon dioxide were not removed it would cause the cross-country runner to fatigue, so they would have to slow down to recover.

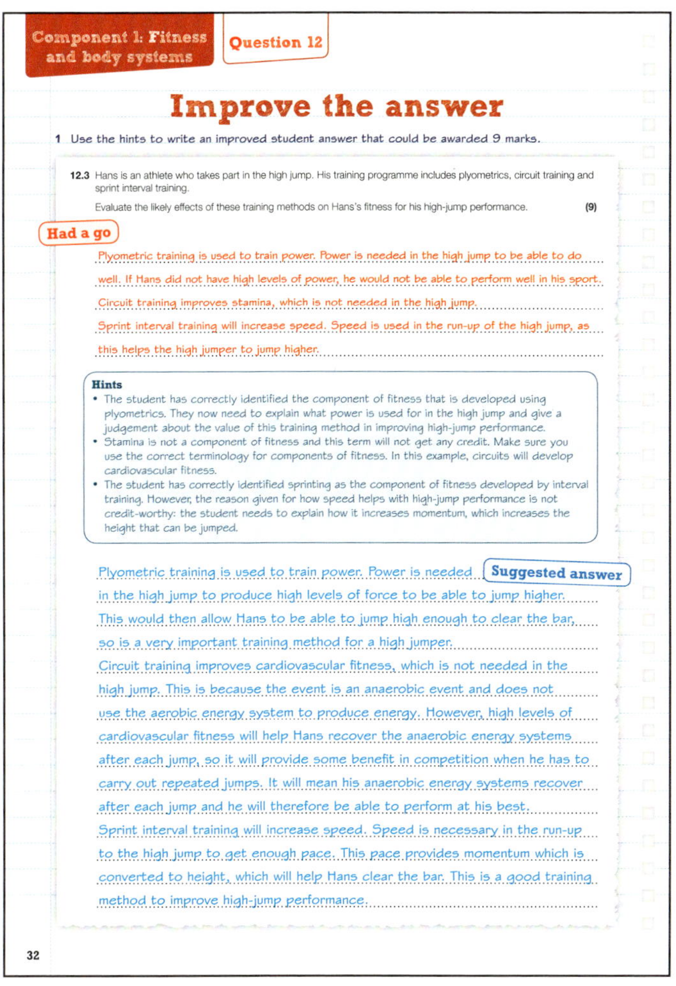

Improve the answer

1 Use the hints to write an improved student answer that could be awarded 9 marks.

12.3 Hans is an athlete who takes part in the high jump. His training programme includes plyometrics, circuit training and sprint interval training.

Evaluate the likely effects of these training methods on Hans's fitness for his high-jump performance. **(9)**

Had a go

Plyometric training is used to train power. Power is needed in the high jump to be able to do well. If Hans did not have high levels of power, he would not be able to perform well in his sport.

Circuit training improves stamina, which is not needed in the high jump.

Sprint interval training will increase speed. Speed is used in the run-up of the high jump, as this helps the high jumper to jump higher.

Hints
- The student has correctly identified the component of fitness that is developed using plyometrics. They now need to explain what power is used for in the high jump and give a judgement about the value of this training method in improving high-jump performance.
- Stamina is not a component of fitness and this term will not get any credit. Make sure you use the correct terminology for components of fitness. In this example, circuits will develop cardiovascular fitness.
- The student has correctly identified sprinting as the component of fitness developed by interval training. However, the reason given for how speed helps with high-jump performance is not credit-worthy: the student needs to explain how it increases momentum, which increases the height that can be jumped.

Suggested answer

Plyometric training is used to train power. Power is needed in the high jump to produce high levels of force to be able to jump higher. This would then allow Hans to be able to jump high enough to clear the bar, so is a very important training method for a high jumper.
Circuit training improves cardiovascular fitness, which is not needed in the high jump. This is because the event is an anaerobic event and does not use the aerobic energy system to produce energy. However, high levels of cardiovascular fitness will help Hans recover the anaerobic energy systems after each jump, so it will provide some benefit in competition when he has to carry out repeated jumps. It will mean his anaerobic energy systems recover after each jump and he will therefore be able to perform at his best.
Sprint interval training will increase speed. Speed is necessary in the run-up to the high jump to get enough pace. This pace provides momentum which is converted to height, which will help Hans clear the bar. This is a good training method to improve high-jump performance.

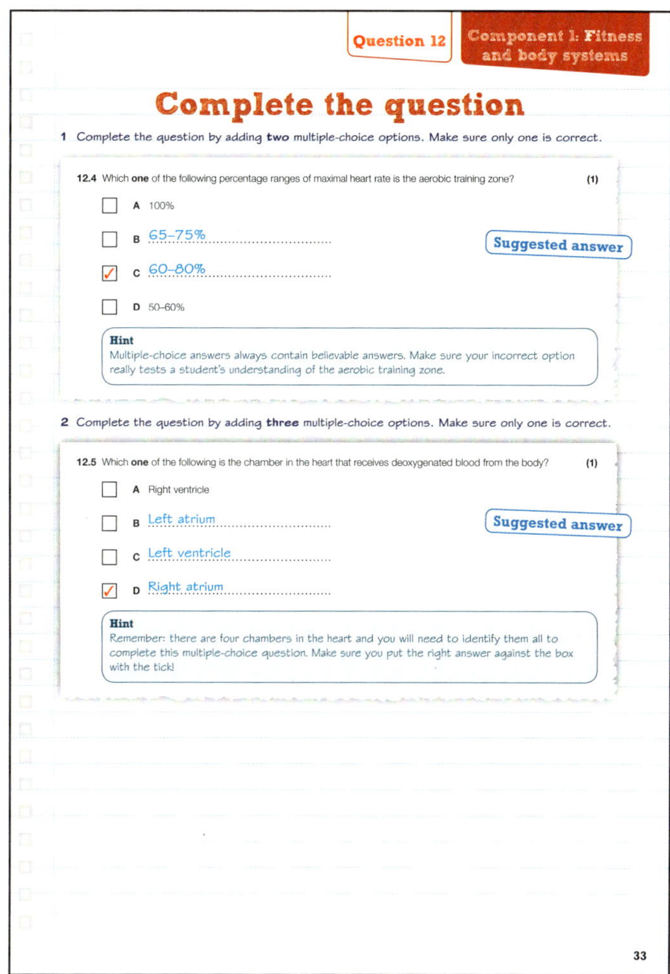

Complete the question

1 Complete the question by adding **two** multiple-choice options. Make sure only one is correct.

12.4 Which **one** of the following percentage ranges of maximal heart rate is the aerobic training zone? **(1)**

- [ ] A 100%
- [ ] B 65–75% — **Suggested answer**
- [✓] C 60–80%
- [ ] D 50–60%

Hint
Multiple-choice answers always contain believable answers. Make sure your incorrect option really tests a student's understanding of the aerobic training zone.

2 Complete the question by adding **three** multiple-choice options. Make sure only one is correct.

12.5 Which **one** of the following is the chamber in the heart that receives deoxygenated blood from the body? **(1)**

- [ ] A Right ventricle
- [ ] B Left atrium — **Suggested answer**
- [ ] C Left ventricle
- [✓] D Right atrium

Hint
Remember: there are four chambers in the heart and you will need to identify them all to complete this multiple-choice question. Make sure you put the right answer against the box with the tick!

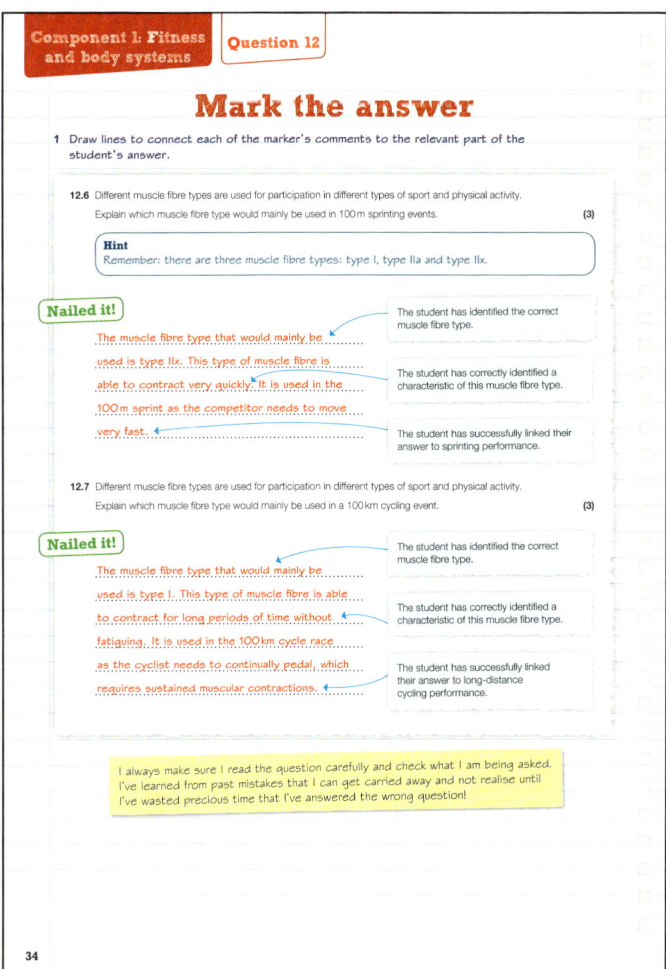

Mark the answer

1 Draw lines to connect each of the marker's comments to the relevant part of the student's answer.

12.6 Different muscle fibre types are used for participation in different types of sport and physical activity.
Explain which muscle fibre type would mainly be used in 100 m sprinting events. **(3)**

Hint
Remember: there are three muscle fibre types: type I, type IIa and type IIx.

Nailed it!

The muscle fibre type that would mainly be used is type IIx. This type of muscle fibre is able to contract very quickly. It is used in the 100 m sprint as the competitor needs to move very fast.

- The student has identified the correct muscle fibre type.
- The student has correctly identified a characteristic of this muscle fibre type.
- The student has successfully linked their answer to sprinting performance.

12.7 Different muscle fibre types are used for participation in different types of sport and physical activity.
Explain which muscle fibre type would mainly be used in a 100 km cycling event. **(3)**

Nailed it!

The muscle fibre type that would mainly be used is type I. This type of muscle fibre is able to contract for long periods of time without fatiguing. It is used in the 100 km cycle race as the cyclist needs to continually pedal, which requires sustained muscular contractions.

- The student has identified the correct muscle fibre type.
- The student has correctly identified a characteristic of this muscle fibre type.
- The student has successfully linked their answer to long-distance cycling performance.

I always make sure I read the question carefully and check what I am being asked. I've learned from past mistakes that I can get carried away and not realise until I've wasted precious time that I've answered the wrong question!

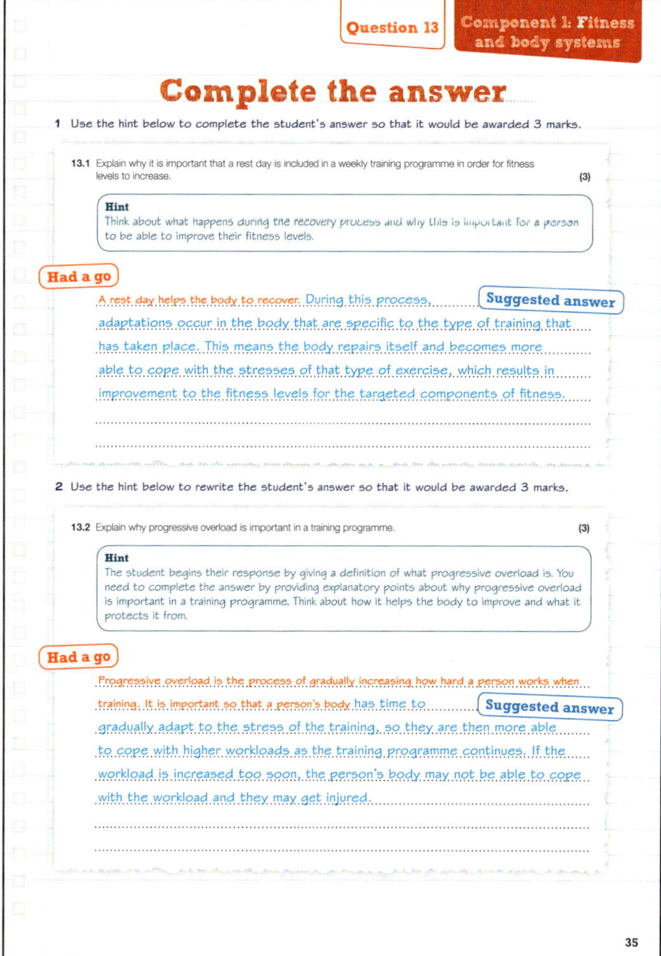

Complete the answer

1 Use the hint below to complete the student's answer so that it would be awarded 3 marks.

13.1 Explain why it is important that a rest day is included in a weekly training programme in order for fitness levels to increase. **(3)**

Hint
Think about what happens during the recovery process and why this is important for a person to be able to improve their fitness levels.

Had a go

A rest day helps the body to recover. During this process, adaptations occur in the body that are specific to the type of training that has taken place. This means the body repairs itself and becomes more able to cope with the stresses of that type of exercise, which results in improvement to the fitness levels for the targeted components of fitness. — **Suggested answer**

2 Use the hint below to rewrite the student's answer so that it would be awarded 3 marks.

13.2 Explain why progressive overload is important in a training programme. **(3)**

Hint
The student begins their response by giving a definition of what progressive overload is. You need to complete the answer by providing explanatory points about why progressive overload is important in a training programme. Think about how it helps the body to improve and what it protects it from.

Had a go

Progressive overload is the process of gradually increasing how hard a person works when training. It is important so that a person's body has time to gradually adapt to the stress of the training, so they are then more able to cope with higher workloads as the training programme continues. If the workload is increased too soon, the person's body may not be able to cope with the workload and they may get injured. — **Suggested answer**

Component 1: Fitness and body systems — Question 13

Improve the answer

1 Use the hint below to write an improved student answer that would be awarded 3 marks.

13.3 Movement in physical activities and sport occurs in different planes.

Figure 8 shows a gymnast performing a star jump.

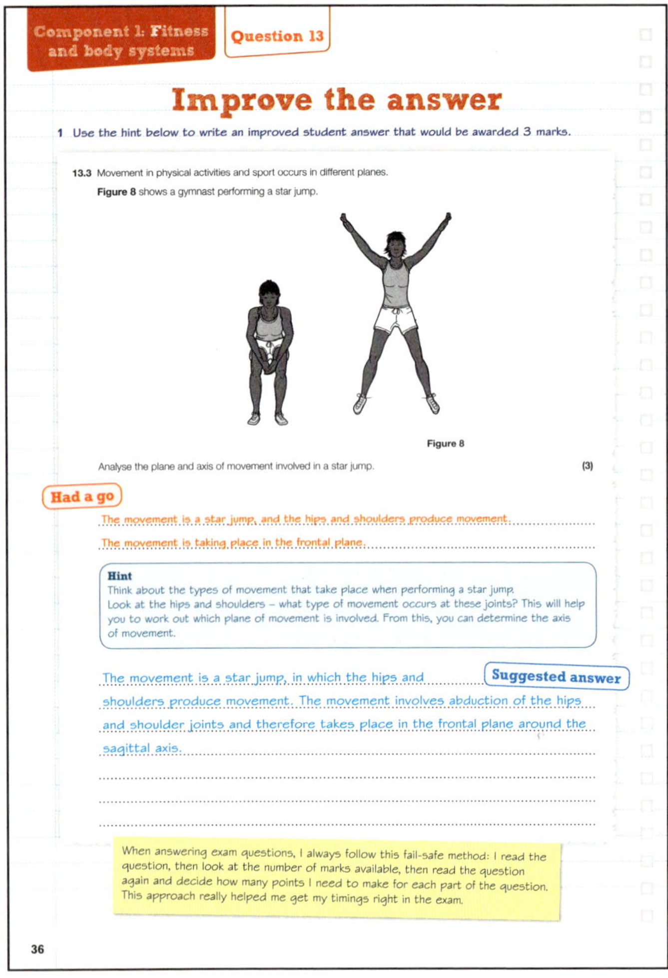

Figure 8

Analyse the plane and axis of movement involved in a star jump. (3)

Had a go

The movement is a star jump, and the hips and shoulders produce movement.

The movement is taking place in the frontal plane.

Hint
Think about the types of movement that take place when performing a star jump.
Look at the hips and shoulders – what type of movement occurs at these joints? This will help
you to work out which plane of movement is involved. From this, you can determine the axis
of movement.

Suggested answer
The movement is a star jump, in which the hips and
shoulders produce movement. The movement involves abduction of the hips
and shoulder joints and therefore takes place in the frontal plane around the
sagittal axis.

When answering exam questions, I always follow this fail-safe method: I read the
question, then look at the number of marks available, then read the question
again and decide how many points I need to make for each part of the question.
This approach really helped me get my timings right in the exam.

Question 13 — Component 1: Fitness and body systems

Complete the question

1 Use the hint below to write an improved student answer that would be awarded 3 marks.

13.4 Figure 9 shows a person **preparing** to kick a rugby ball.

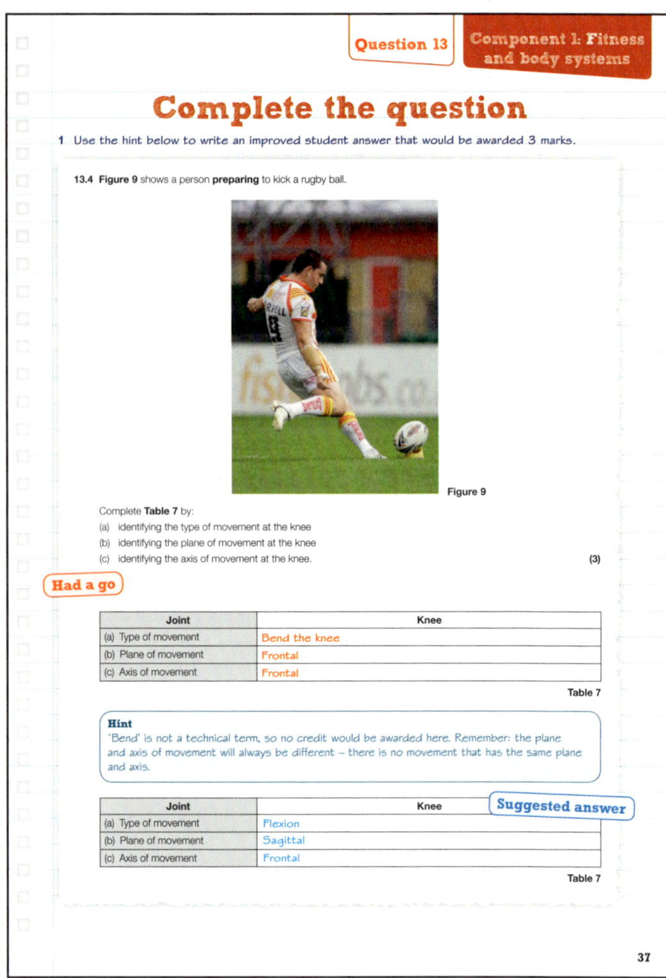

Figure 9

Complete **Table 7** by:
(a) identifying the type of movement at the knee
(b) identifying the plane of movement at the knee
(c) identifying the axis of movement at the knee. (3)

Had a go

Joint	Knee
(a) Type of movement	Bend the knee
(b) Plane of movement	Frontal
(c) Axis of movement	Frontal

Table 7

Hint
'Bend' is not a technical term, so no credit would be awarded here. Remember: the plane
and axis of movement will always be different – there is no movement that has the same plane
and axis.

Suggested answer

Joint	Knee
(a) Type of movement	Flexion
(b) Plane of movement	Sagittal
(c) Axis of movement	Frontal

Table 7

Component 1: Fitness and body systems — Question 13

Find the answer

1 Use the mark scheme to find the answer that would be awarded 4 marks. Choose **A, B** or **C**.

13.5 Analyse the role of red blood cells for long-distance cycling. (4)

Question	Answer	Mark
13.5	(1) mark for each point up to 4 marks. Red blood cells carry oxygen (1) as they contain haemoglobin, which binds oxygen (1). Oxygen is needed by the aerobic energy system (1), which is the main method of supplying ATP during long-distance cycling (1).	4

Hint
Remember to check each answer against the mark scheme closely to make sure it covers all
four points, otherwise the answer can't be awarded the full 4 marks.

A Oxygen is transported in the red blood cells because they have haemoglobin. A
long-distance cyclist will supply ATP using the aerobic energy system, so they need
high levels of oxygen.

B Red blood cells contain haemoglobin. Oxygen is carried by haemoglobin, so the more
red blood cells there are in the blood the more oxygen can be carried. Oxygen is
used for the aerobic energy system. A long-distance cyclist needs lots of energy.

C The aerobic energy system supplies most of a long-distance cyclist's ATP. The
aerobic energy system requires high levels of oxygen. Red blood cells carry oxygen
because they contain haemoglobin, which binds oxygen to it. So having high levels
of red blood cells means there is a lot of oxygen for ATP production by the aerobic
energy system.

Hint
Make sure the link to sporting performance is clearly related to the function of red blood
cells. You would not gain any marks for simply saying 'they provide oxygen' or 'they produce
energy': you need to explain what the red blood cell provides and how this benefits
cycling performance.

Suggested answer
Answer C would be awarded full marks because the aerobic
energy system has been identified as the main energy system to produce ATP
for the cyclist. High levels of oxygen have been stated as being needed for
this system to work well. The fact that red blood cells carry oxygen has been
identified, which has also been linked to how they carry oxygen by having
haemoglobin, which binds to oxygen.

Question 13 — Component 1: Fitness and body systems

Complete the answer

1 Complete the student's answer so that it would be awarded 3 marks.

13.6 Explain why a person should take part in an active cool down after completing sport and physical activity. (3)

Had a go

A cool down is necessary to help reduce muscle soreness after taking part in exercise.
It does this by helping to get rid of lactic acid from the
body. It also slowly decreases heart rate back to resting levels. **Suggested answer**

Hint
This student's answer only gives one reason why a cool down is useful to the body.
The student also needs to:
• explain what a cool down does to heart rate
• explain how taking part in a cool down can help to remove the waste product that causes
  muscle soreness.

2 Complete the student's answer so that it would be awarded 4 marks.

13.7 Explain why a shot-put thrower may be tempted to take anabolic steroids to improve their performance. (4)

Hint
The student starts their answer by stating what anabolic steroids do to muscle tissues
and how this would impact on muscle strength. To complete the student's answer, you need
to apply this physiological benefit to how taking anabolic steroids would improve shot-put
throwing performance.

Had a go

Anabolic steroids increase the rate at which muscle tissue grows, helping to increase muscle
strength. A shot-put thrower may take anabolic steroids to get bigger **Suggested answer**
muscles, which would help them to throw the shot-put further. This would be
beneficial for a shot-put thrower as they need high levels of power – a product
of strength and speed – to throw the shot-put a long distance.

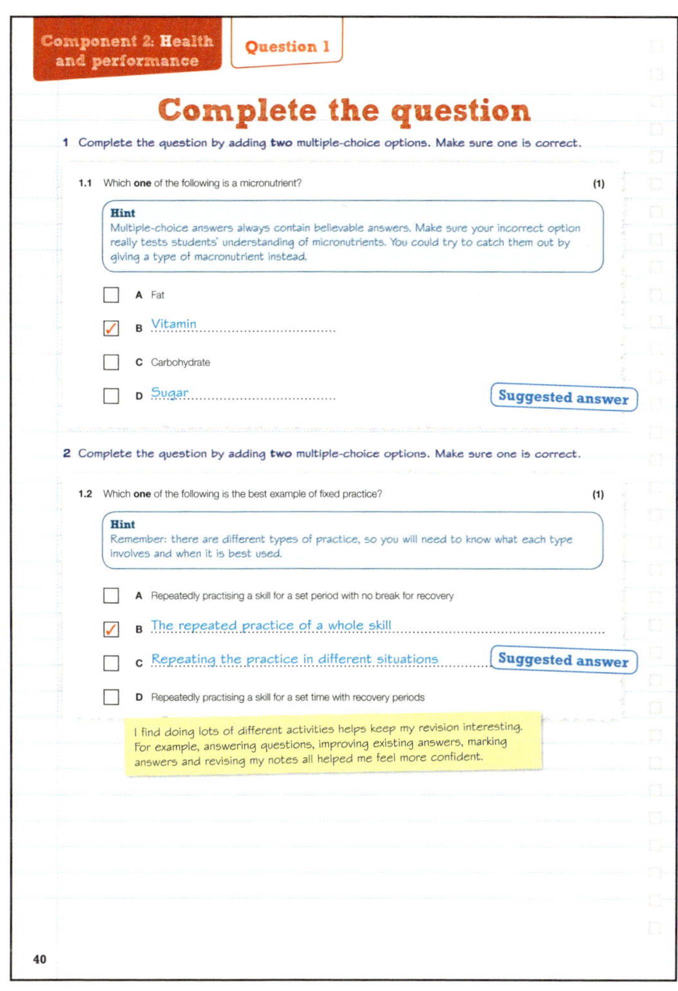

Component 2: Health and performance — Question 1

Complete the question

1 Complete the question by adding **two** multiple-choice options. Make sure one is correct.

1.1 Which **one** of the following is a micronutrient? (1)

> **Hint**
> Multiple-choice answers always contain believable answers. Make sure your incorrect option really tests students' understanding of micronutrients. You could try to catch them out by giving a type of macronutrient instead.

- [ ] **A** Fat
- [x] **B** Vitamin .... *Suggested answer*
- [ ] **C** Carbohydrate
- [ ] **D** Sugar

2 Complete the question by adding **two** multiple-choice options. Make sure one is correct.

1.2 Which **one** of the following is the best example of fixed practice? (1)

> **Hint**
> Remember: there are different types of practice, so you will need to know what each type involves and when it is best used.

- [ ] **A** Repeatedly practising a skill for a set period with no break for recovery
- [x] **B** The repeated practice of a whole skill
- [ ] **C** Repeating the practice in different situations *Suggested answer*
- [ ] **D** Repeatedly practising a skill for a set time with recovery periods

> I find doing lots of different activities helps keep my revision interesting. For example, answering questions, improving existing answers, marking answers and revising my notes all helped me feel more confident.

40

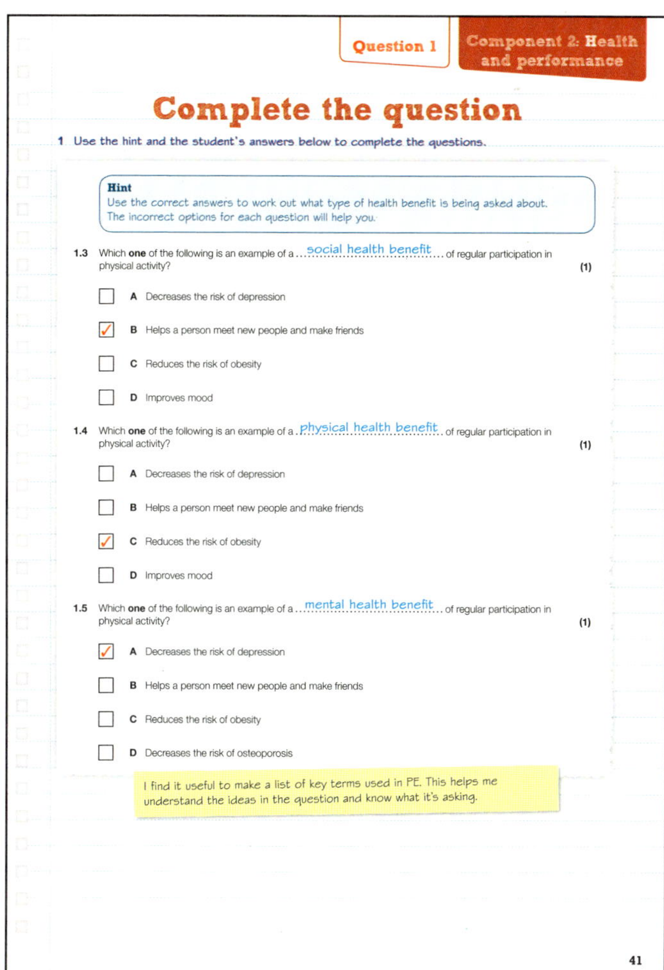

Question 1 — Component 2: Health and performance

Complete the question

1 Use the hint and the student's answers below to complete the questions.

> **Hint**
> Use the correct answers to work out what type of health benefit is being asked about. The incorrect options for each question will help you.

1.3 Which **one** of the following is an example of a ...social health benefit... of regular participation in physical activity? (1)

- [ ] **A** Decreases the risk of depression
- [x] **B** Helps a person meet new people and make friends
- [ ] **C** Reduces the risk of obesity
- [ ] **D** Improves mood

1.4 Which **one** of the following is an example of a ...physical health benefit... of regular participation in physical activity? (1)

- [ ] **A** Decreases the risk of depression
- [ ] **B** Helps a person meet new people and make friends
- [x] **C** Reduces the risk of obesity
- [ ] **D** Improves mood

1.5 Which **one** of the following is an example of a ...mental health benefit... of regular participation in physical activity? (1)

- [x] **A** Decreases the risk of depression
- [ ] **B** Helps a person meet new people and make friends
- [ ] **C** Reduces the risk of obesity
- [ ] **D** Decreases the risk of osteoporosis

> I find it useful to make a list of key terms used in PE. This helps me understand the ideas in the question and know what it's asking.

41

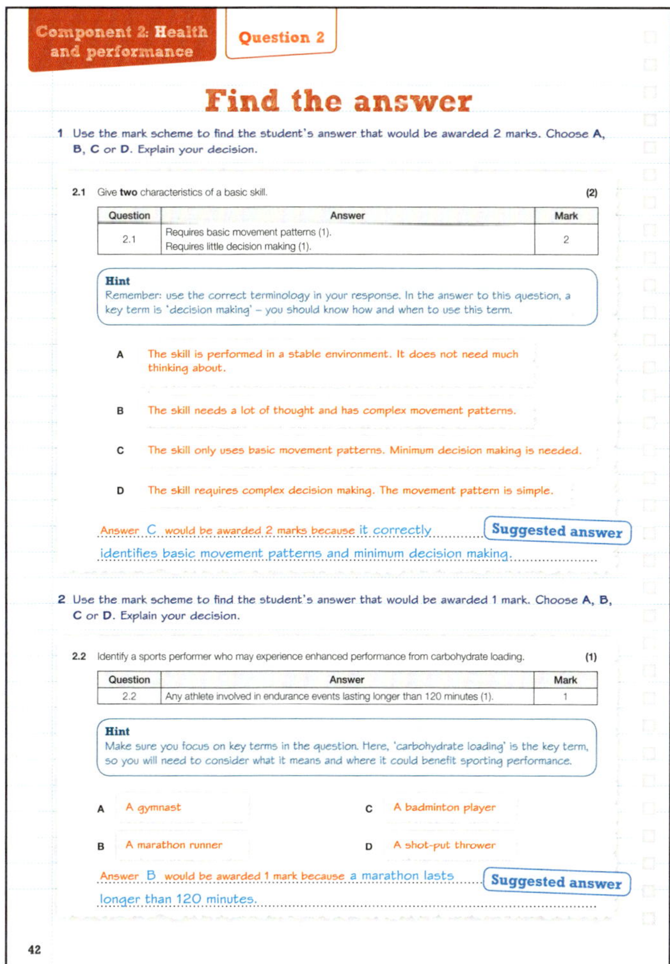

Component 2: Health and performance — Question 2

Find the answer

1 Use the mark scheme to find the student's answer that would be awarded 2 marks. Choose A, B, C or D. Explain your decision.

2.1 Give **two** characteristics of a basic skill. (2)

Question	Answer	Mark
2.1	Requires basic movement patterns (1). Requires little decision making (1).	2

> **Hint**
> Remember: use the correct terminology in your response. In the answer to this question, a key term is 'decision making' – you should know how and when to use this term.

A The skill is performed in a stable environment. It does not need much thinking about.

B The skill needs a lot of thought and has complex movement patterns.

C The skill only uses basic movement patterns. Minimum decision making is needed.

D The skill requires complex decision making. The movement pattern is simple.

Answer C would be awarded 2 marks because it correctly identifies basic movement patterns and minimum decision making. *Suggested answer*

2 Use the mark scheme to find the student's answer that would be awarded 1 mark. Choose A, B, C or D. Explain your decision.

2.2 Identify a sports performer who may experience enhanced performance from carbohydrate loading. (1)

Question	Answer	Mark
2.2	Any athlete involved in endurance events lasting longer than 120 minutes (1).	1

> **Hint**
> Make sure you focus on key terms in the question. Here, 'carbohydrate loading' is the key term, so you will need to consider what it means and where it could benefit sporting performance.

A A gymnast   **C** A badminton player

B A marathon runner   **D** A shot-put thrower

Answer B would be awarded 1 mark because a marathon lasts longer than 120 minutes. *Suggested answer*

42

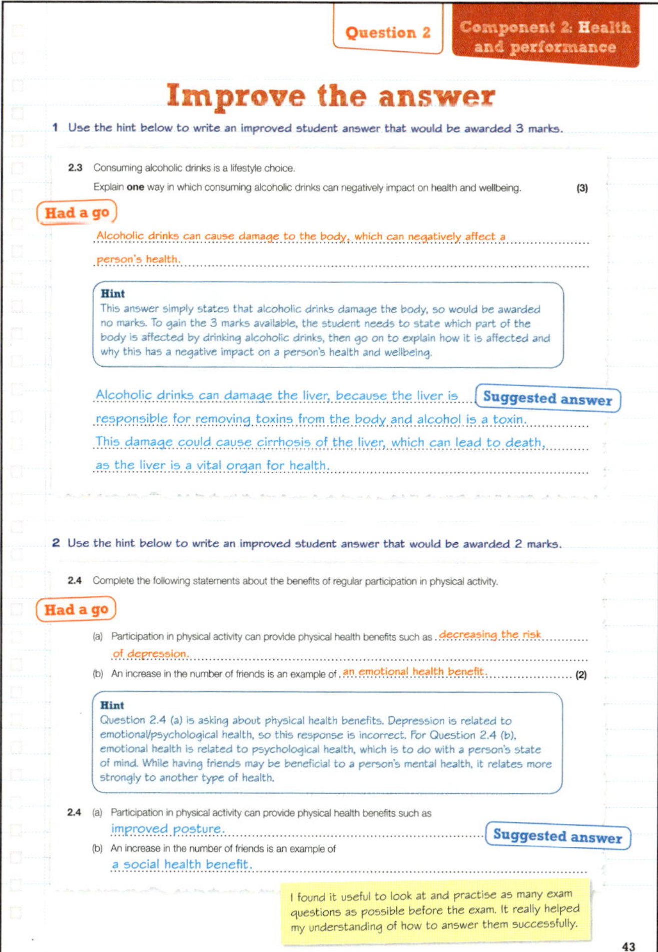

Question 2 — Component 2: Health and performance

Improve the answer

1 Use the hint below to write an improved student answer that would be awarded 3 marks.

2.3 Consuming alcoholic drinks is a lifestyle choice.

Explain **one** way in which consuming alcoholic drinks can negatively impact on health and wellbeing. (3)

Had a go

Alcoholic drinks can cause damage to the body, which can negatively affect a person's health.

> **Hint**
> This answer simply states that alcoholic drinks damage the body, so would be awarded no marks. To gain the 3 marks available, the student needs to state which part of the body is affected by drinking alcoholic drinks, then go on to explain how it is affected and why this has a negative impact on a person's health and wellbeing.

Alcoholic drinks can damage the liver, because the liver is responsible for removing toxins from the body and alcohol is a toxin. This damage could cause cirrhosis of the liver, which can lead to death, as the liver is a vital organ for health. *Suggested answer*

2 Use the hint below to write an improved student answer that would be awarded 2 marks.

2.4 Complete the following statements about the benefits of regular participation in physical activity.

Had a go

(a) Participation in physical activity can provide physical health benefits such as ...decreasing the risk of depression.

(b) An increase in the number of friends is an example of ...an emotional health benefit. (2)

> **Hint**
> Question 2.4 (a) is asking about physical health benefits. Depression is related to emotional/psychological health, so this response is incorrect. For Question 2.4 (b), emotional health is related to psychological health, which is to do with a person's state of mind. While having friends may be beneficial to a person's mental health, it relates more strongly to another type of health.

2.4 (a) Participation in physical activity can provide physical health benefits such as improved posture. *Suggested answer*

(b) An increase in the number of friends is an example of a social health benefit.

> I found it useful to look at and practise as many exam questions as possible before the exam. It really helped my understanding of how to answer them successfully.

43

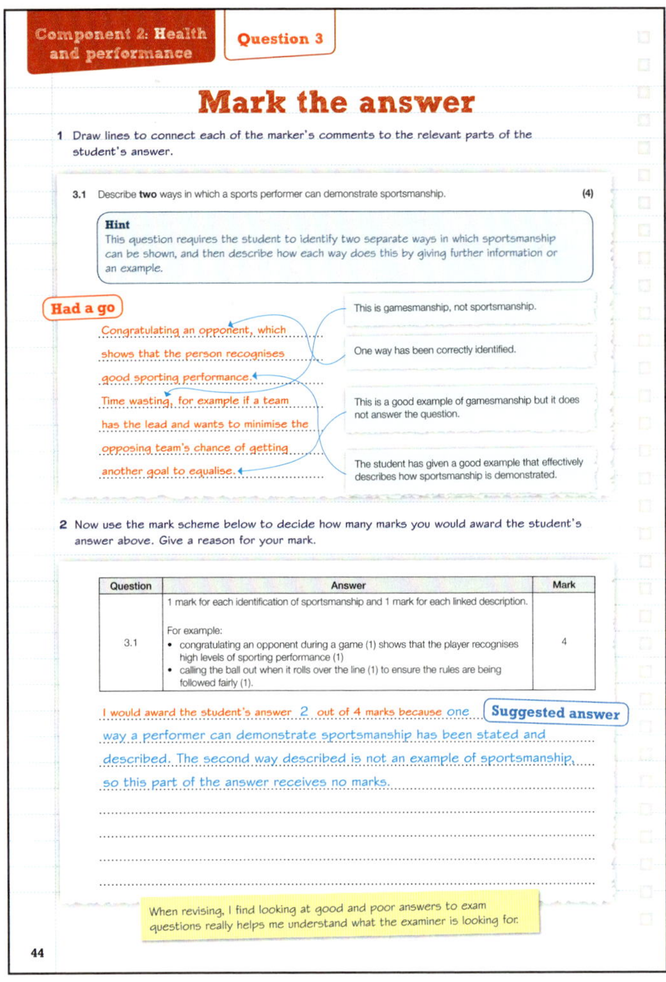

Mark the answer

1 Draw lines to connect each of the marker's comments to the relevant parts of the student's answer.

3.1 Describe **two** ways in which a sports performer can demonstrate sportsmanship. (4)

Hint
This question requires the student to identify two separate ways in which sportsmanship can be shown, and then describe how each way does this by giving further information or an example.

Had a go

Congratulating an opponent, which shows that the person recognises good sporting performance.

Time wasting, for example if a team has the lead and wants to minimise the opposing team's chance of getting another goal to equalise.

Marker comments:
- This is gamesmanship, not sportsmanship.
- One way has been correctly identified.
- This is a good example of gamesmanship but it does not answer the question.
- The student has given a good example that effectively describes how sportsmanship is demonstrated.

2 Now use the mark scheme below to decide how many marks you would award the student's answer above. Give a reason for your mark.

Question	Answer	Mark
3.1	1 mark for each identification of sportsmanship and 1 mark for each linked description. For example: • congratulating an opponent during a game (1) shows that the player recognises high levels of sporting performance (1) • calling the ball out when it rolls over the line (1) to ensure the rules are being followed fairly (1).	4

Suggested answer

I would award the student's answer 2 out of 4 marks because one way a performer can demonstrate sportsmanship has been stated and described. The second way described is not an example of sportsmanship, so this part of the answer receives no marks.

When revising, I find looking at good and poor answers to exam questions really helps me understand what the examiner is looking for.

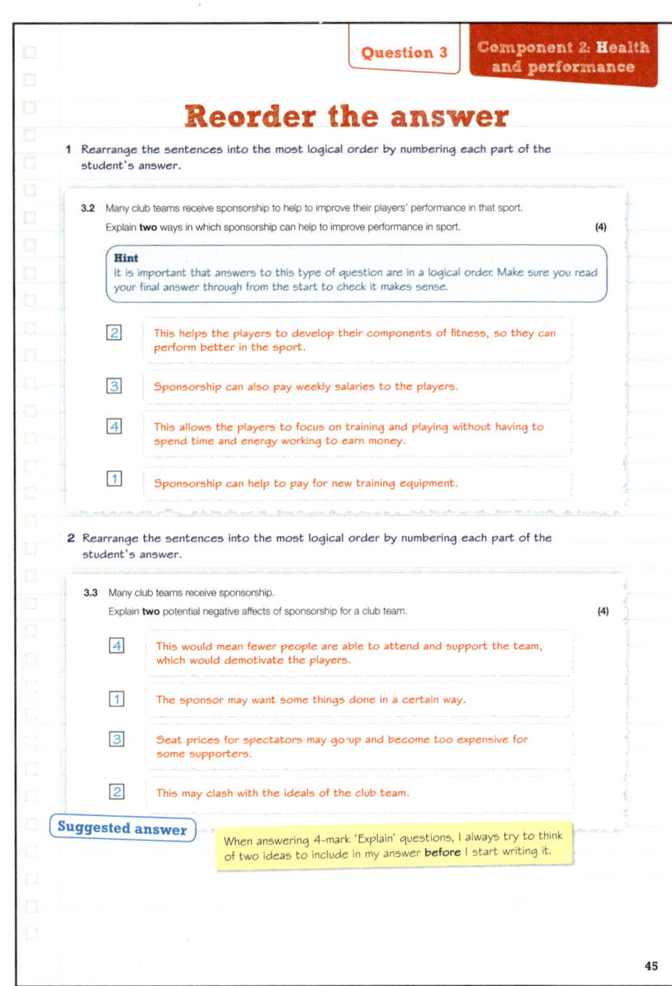

Reorder the answer

1 Rearrange the sentences into the most logical order by numbering each part of the student's answer.

3.2 Many club teams receive sponsorship to help to improve their players' performance in that sport.

Explain **two** ways in which sponsorship can help to improve performance in sport. (4)

Hint
It is important that answers to this type of question are in a logical order. Make sure you read your final answer through from the start to check it makes sense.

2. This helps the players to develop their components of fitness, so they can perform better in the sport.

3. Sponsorship can also pay weekly salaries to the players.

4. This allows the players to focus on training and playing without having to spend time and energy working to earn money.

1. Sponsorship can help to pay for new training equipment.

2 Rearrange the sentences into the most logical order by numbering each part of the student's answer.

3.3 Many club teams receive sponsorship.

Explain **two** potential negative affects of sponsorship for a club team. (4)

4. This would mean fewer people are able to attend and support the team, which would demotivate the players.

1. The sponsor may want some things done in a certain way.

3. Seat prices for spectators may go up and become too expensive for some supporters.

2. This may clash with the ideals of the club team.

Suggested answer

When answering 4-mark 'Explain' questions, I always try to think of two ideas to include in my answer **before** I start writing it.

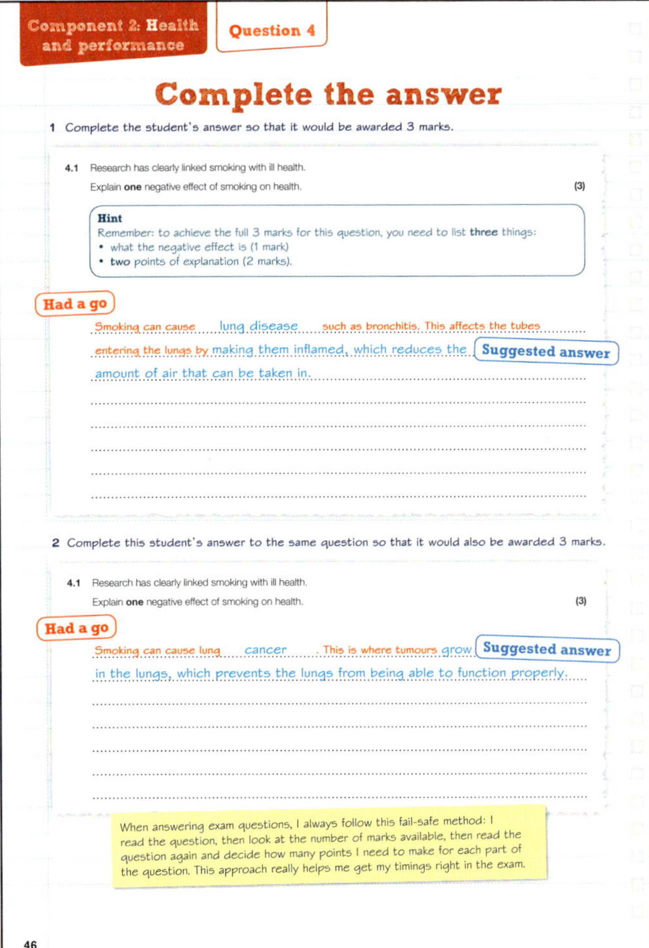

Complete the answer

1 Complete the student's answer so that it would be awarded 3 marks.

4.1 Research has clearly linked smoking with ill health.

Explain **one** negative effect of smoking on health. (3)

Hint
Remember: to achieve the full 3 marks for this question, you need to list **three** things:
• what the negative effect is (1 mark)
• **two** points of explanation (2 marks).

Had a go

Smoking can cause lung disease such as bronchitis. This affects the tubes entering the lungs by making them inflamed, which reduces the **Suggested answer** amount of air that can be taken in.

2 Complete this student's answer to the same question so that it would also be awarded 3 marks.

4.1 Research has clearly linked smoking with ill health.

Explain **one** negative effect of smoking on health. (3)

Had a go

Smoking can cause lung cancer. This is where tumours grow **Suggested answer** in the lungs, which prevents the lungs from being able to function properly.

When answering exam questions, I always follow this fail-safe method: I read the question, then look at the number of marks available, then read the question again and decide how many points I need to make for each part of the question. This approach really helps me get my timings right in the exam.

Improve the answer

1 Use the hint below to improve the student's answer so that it would be awarded 3 marks.

4.2 Explain what is meant by coronary heart disease. (3)

Had a go

Coronary heart disease is where the blood vessels that supply blood to the heart do not work properly. This can occur because of a high-fat diet.

Hint
To achieve 3 marks for this question you need to list **three** things:
• what coronary heart disease is – this student's answer gives a partial definition and needs to be more specific about how the blood vessels supplying the heart do not work properly
• **two points of explanation** about how coronary heart disease occurs – this student has made one point but needs to go on to explain how a high-fat diet contributes to coronary heart disease.

Suggested answer

Coronary heart disease is where the blood vessels that supply blood to the heart become blocked, preventing blood from reaching the heart. This can occur because of a high-fat diet, which causes plaques to form in the coronary blood vessels.

2 Use the hint below to improve the student's answer so that it would be awarded 3 marks.

4.3 Explain what is meant by type 1 diabetes. (3)

Had a go

Type 1 diabetes is where blood sugar levels get too high and the person needs medicine to control it.

Hint
The student has correctly described what type 1 diabetes is. While they have stated that medicine is needed to control it, they have not specified what the medicine is. Finally, a further point needs to be made about what the medicine does/why it is needed.

Suggested answer

Type 1 diabetes is where a person cannot control their blood sugar levels because the pancreas does not produce enough insulin. This is very damaging for the body, so diabetics need insulin injections to remove the excess sugar from the blood.

I really took the time to learn key terms used in PE, and even created flash cards to help me learn key words when revising. It meant I always knew what a question was asking me in the exam and could use the terms accurately in my answers, too.

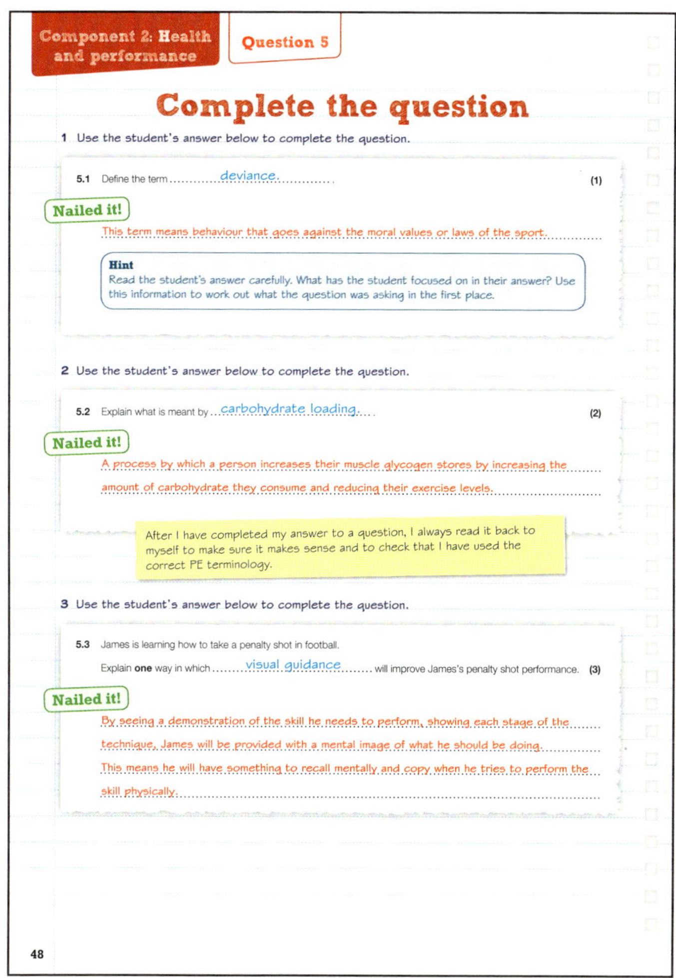

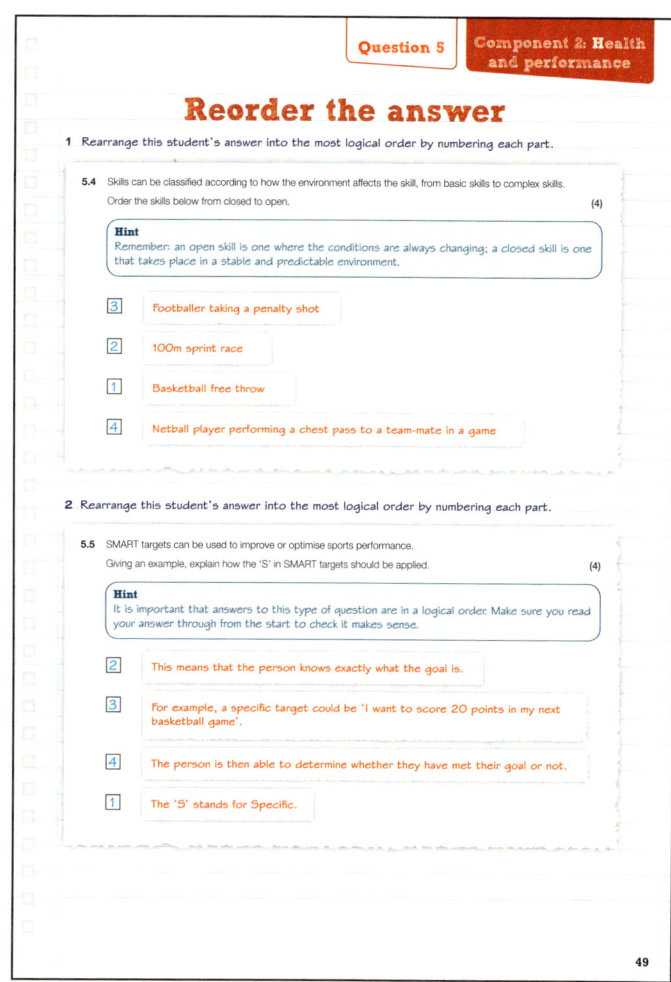

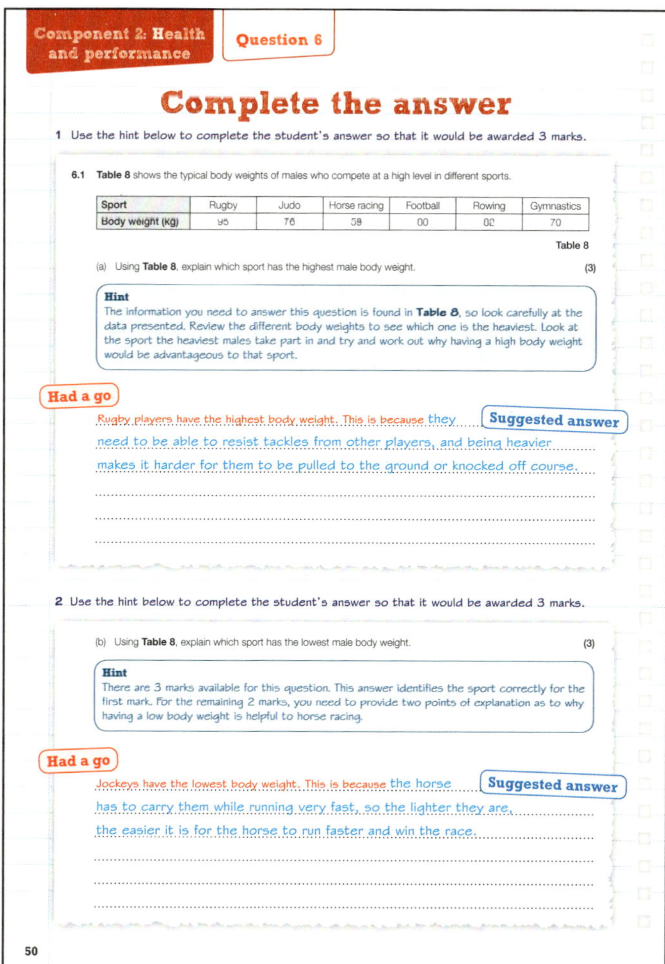

Sport	Rugby	Judo	Horse racing	Football	Rowing	Gymnastics
Body weight (kg)	95	78	58	80	82	70

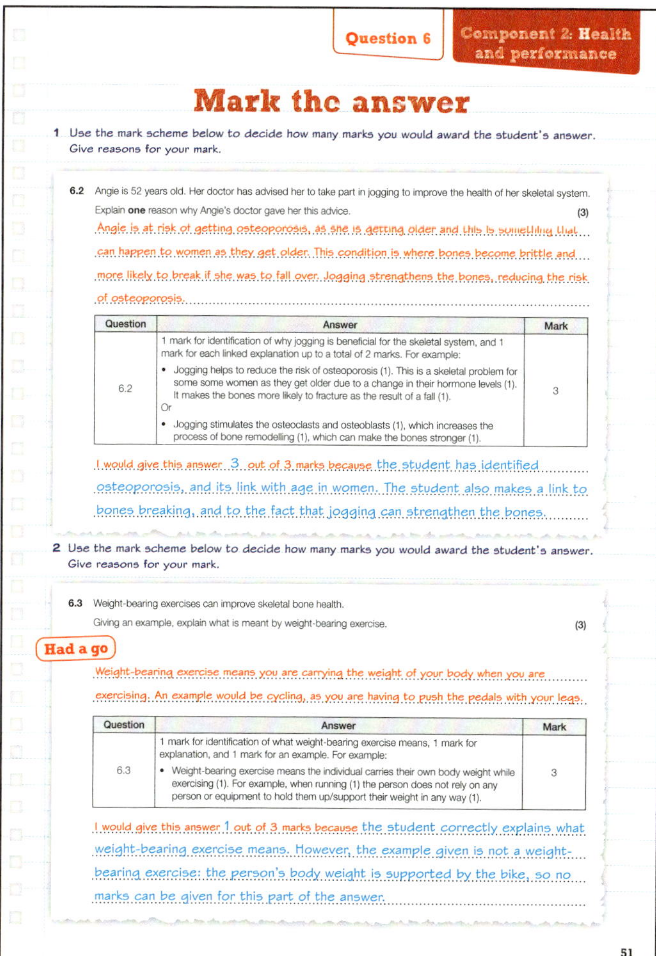

Question	Answer	Mark
6.2	1 mark for identification of why jogging is beneficial for the skeletal system, and 1 mark for each linked explanation up to a total of 2 marks. For example: • Jogging helps to reduce the risk of osteoporosis (1). This is a skeletal problem for some some women as they get older due to a change in their hormone levels (1). It makes the bones more likely to fracture as the result of a fall (1). Or • Jogging stimulates the osteoclasts and osteoblasts (1), which increases the process of bone remodelling (1), which can make the bones stronger (1).	3

Question	Answer	Mark
6.3	1 mark for identification of what weight-bearing exercise means, 1 mark for explanation, and 1 mark for an example. For example: • Weight-bearing exercise means the individual carries their own body weight while exercising (1). For example, when running (1) the person does not rely on any person or equipment to hold them up/support their weight in any way (1).	3

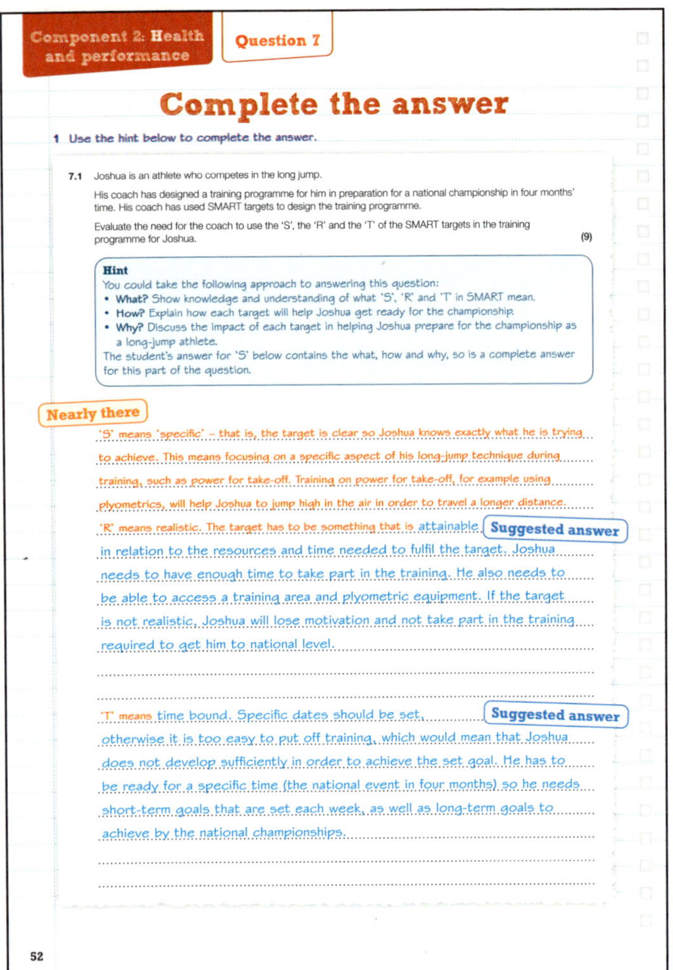

Complete the answer

1 Use the hint below to complete the answer.

7.1 Joshua is an athlete who competes in the long jump.

His coach has designed a training programme for him in preparation for a national championship in four months' time. His coach has used SMART targets to design the training programme.

Evaluate the need for the coach to use the 'S', the 'R' and the 'T' of the SMART targets in the training programme for Joshua. **(9)**

Hint
You could take the following approach to answering this question:
- **What?** Show knowledge and understanding of what 'S', 'R' and 'T' in SMART mean.
- **How?** Explain how each target will help Joshua get ready for the championship.
- **Why?** Discuss the impact of each target in helping Joshua prepare for the championship as a long-jump athlete.

The student's answer for 'S' below contains the what, how and why, so is a complete answer for this part of the question.

Nearly there

'S' means 'specific' – that is, the target is clear so Joshua knows exactly what he is trying to achieve. This means focusing on a specific aspect of his long-jump technique during training, such as power for take-off. Training on power for take-off, for example using plyometrics, will help Joshua to jump high in the air in order to travel a longer distance.

'R' means realistic. The target has to be something that is attainable **[Suggested answer]** in relation to the resources and time needed to fulfil the target. Joshua needs to have enough time to take part in the training. He also needs to be able to access a training area and plyometric equipment. If the target is not realistic, Joshua will lose motivation and not take part in the training required to get him to national level.

'T' means time bound. Specific dates should be set, **[Suggested answer]** otherwise it is too easy to put off training, which would mean that Joshua does not develop sufficiently in order to achieve the set goal. He has to be ready for a specific time (the national event in four months) so he needs short-term goals that are set each week, as well as long-term goals to achieve by the national championships.

52

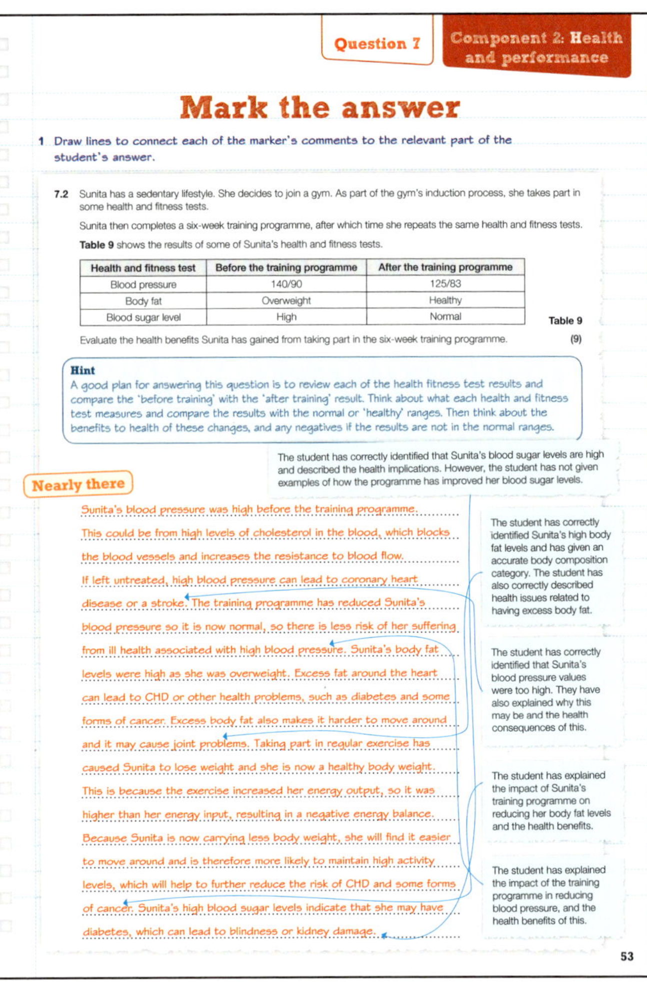

Mark the answer

1 Draw lines to connect each of the marker's comments to the relevant part of the student's answer.

7.2 Sunita has a sedentary lifestyle. She decides to join a gym. As part of the gym's induction process, she takes part in some health and fitness tests.

Sunita then completes a six-week training programme, after which time she repeats the same health and fitness tests.

Table 9 shows the results of some of Sunita's health and fitness tests.

Health and fitness test	Before the training programme	After the training programme
Blood pressure	140/90	125/83
Body fat	Overweight	Healthy
Blood sugar level	High	Normal

Table 9

Evaluate the health benefits Sunita has gained from taking part in the six-week training programme. **(9)**

Hint
A good plan for answering this question is to review each of the health fitness test results and compare the 'before training' with the 'after training' result. Think about what each health and fitness test measures and compare the results with the normal or 'healthy' ranges. Then think about the benefits to health of these changes, and any negatives if the results are not in the normal ranges.

The student has correctly identified that Sunita's blood sugar levels are high and described the health implications. However, the student has not given examples of how the programme has improved her blood sugar levels.

Nearly there

Sunita's blood pressure was high before the training programme. This could be from high levels of cholesterol in the blood, which blocks the blood vessels and increases the resistance to blood flow. If left untreated, high blood pressure can lead to coronary heart disease or a stroke. The training programme has reduced Sunita's blood pressure so it is now normal, so there is less risk of her suffering from ill health associated with high blood pressure. Sunita's body fat levels were high as she was overweight. Excess fat around the heart can lead to CHD or other health problems, such as diabetes and some forms of cancer. Excess body fat also makes it harder to move around and it may cause joint problems. Taking part in regular exercise has caused Sunita to lose weight and she is now at a healthy body weight. This is because the exercise increased her energy output, so it was higher than her energy input, resulting in a negative energy balance. Because Sunita is now carrying less body weight, she will find it easier to move around and is therefore more likely to maintain high activity levels, which will help to further reduce the risk of CHD and some forms of cancer. Sunita's high blood sugar levels indicate that she may have diabetes, which can lead to blindness or kidney damage.

The student has correctly identified Sunita's high body fat levels and has given an accurate body composition category. The student has also correctly described health issues related to having excess body fat.

The student has correctly identified that Sunita's blood pressure values were too high. They have also explained why this may be and the health consequences of this.

The student has explained the impact of Sunita's training programme on reducing her body fat levels and the health benefits.

The student has explained the impact of the training programme in reducing blood pressure, and the health benefits of this.

53

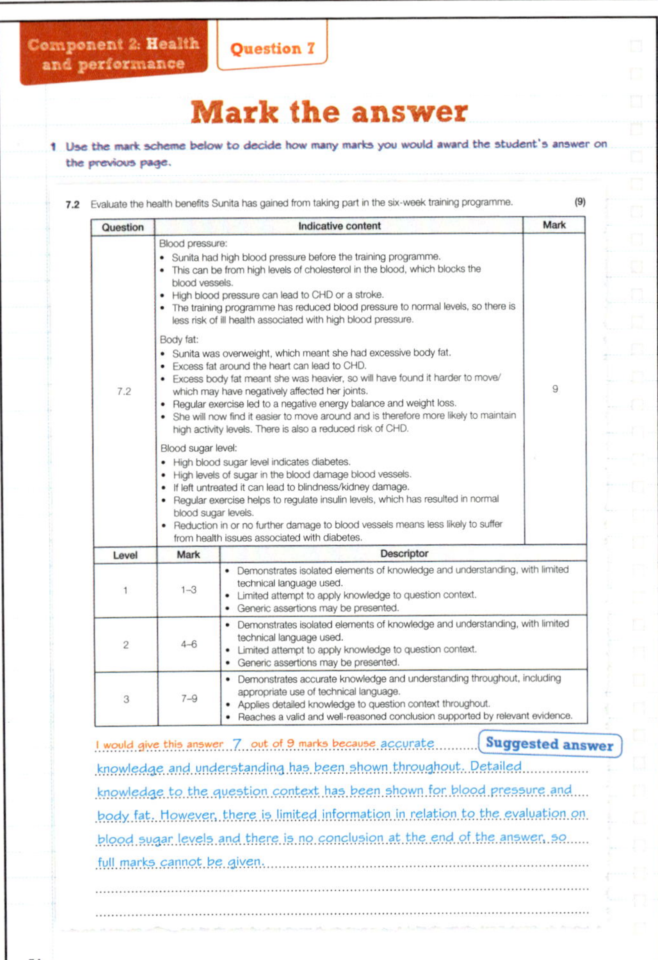

Mark the answer

1 Use the mark scheme below to decide how many marks you would award the student's answer on the previous page.

7.2 Evaluate the health benefits Sunita has gained from taking part in the six-week training programme. **(9)**

Question	Indicative content	Mark
7.2	**Blood pressure:** • Sunita had high blood pressure before the training programme. • This can be from high levels of cholesterol in the blood, which blocks the blood vessels. • High blood pressure can lead to CHD or a stroke. • The training programme has reduced blood pressure to normal levels, so there is less risk of ill health associated with high blood pressure. **Body fat:** • Sunita was overweight, which meant she had excessive body fat. • Excess fat around the heart can lead to CHD. • Excess body fat meant she was heavier, so will have found it harder to move/ which may have negatively affected her joints. • Regular exercise led to a negative energy balance and weight loss. • She will now find it easier to move around and is therefore more likely to maintain high activity levels. There is also a reduced risk of CHD. **Blood sugar level:** • High blood sugar level indicates diabetes. • High levels of sugar in the blood damage blood vessels. • If left untreated it can lead to blindness/kidney damage. • Regular exercise helps to regulate insulin levels, which has resulted in normal blood sugar levels. • Reduction in or no further damage to blood vessels means less likely to suffer from health issues associated with diabetes.	9

Level	Mark	Descriptor
1	1–3	• Demonstrates isolated elements of knowledge and understanding, with limited technical language used. • Limited attempt to apply knowledge to question context. • Generic assertions may be presented.
2	4–6	• Demonstrates isolated elements of knowledge and understanding, with limited technical language used. • Limited attempt to apply knowledge to question context. • Generic assertions may be presented.
3	7–9	• Demonstrates accurate knowledge and understanding throughout, including appropriate use of technical language. • Applies detailed knowledge to question context throughout. • Reaches a valid and well-reasoned conclusion supported by relevant evidence.

I would give this answer 7 out of 9 marks because accurate **[Suggested answer]** knowledge and understanding has been shown throughout. Detailed knowledge to the question context has been shown for blood pressure and body fat. However, there is limited information in relation to the evaluation on blood sugar levels and there is no conclusion at the end of the answer, so full marks cannot be given.

54

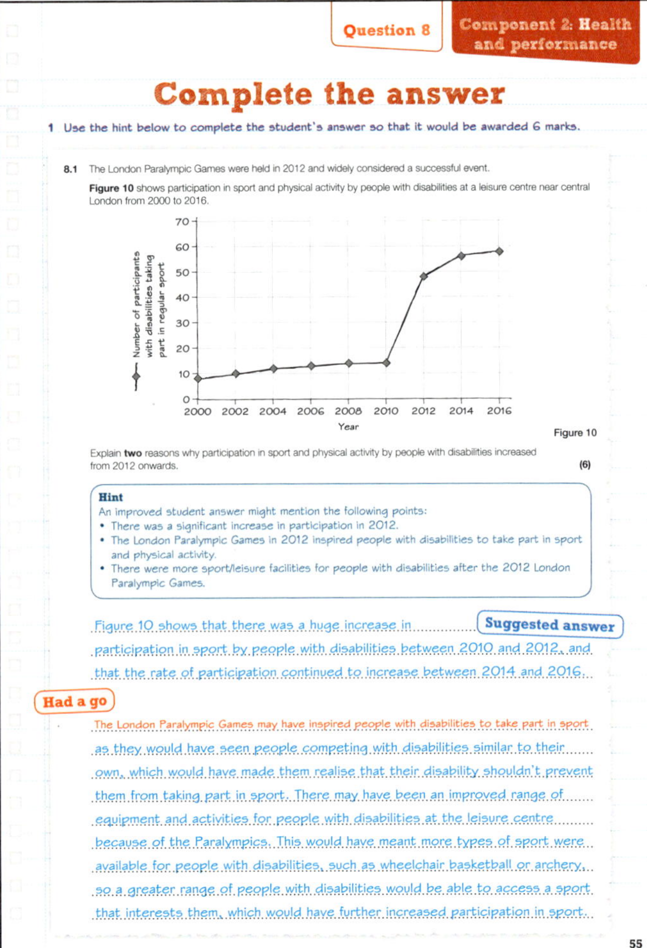

Complete the answer

1 Use the hint below to complete the student's answer so that it would be awarded 6 marks.

8.1 The London Paralympic Games were held in 2012 and widely considered a successful event.

Figure 10 shows participation in sport and physical activity by people with disabilities at a leisure centre near central London from 2000 to 2016.

Figure 10

Explain **two** reasons why participation in sport and physical activity by people with disabilities increased from 2012 onwards. **(6)**

Hint
An improved student answer might mention the following points:
- There was a significant increase in participation in 2012.
- The London Paralympic Games in 2012 inspired people with disabilities to take part in sport and physical activity.
- There were more sport/leisure facilities for people with disabilities after the 2012 London Paralympic Games.

Figure 10 shows that there was a huge increase in **[Suggested answer]** participation in sport by people with disabilities between 2010 and 2012, and that the rate of participation continued to increase between 2014 and 2016.

Had a go

The London Paralympic Games may have inspired people with disabilities to take part in sport as they would have seen people competing with disabilities similar to their own, which would have made them realise that their disability shouldn't prevent them from taking part in sport. There may have been an improved range of equipment and activities for people with disabilities at the leisure centre because of the Paralympics. This would have meant more types of sport were available for people with disabilities, such as wheelchair basketball or archery, so a greater range of people with disabilities would be able to access a sport that interests them, which would have further increased participation in sport.

55

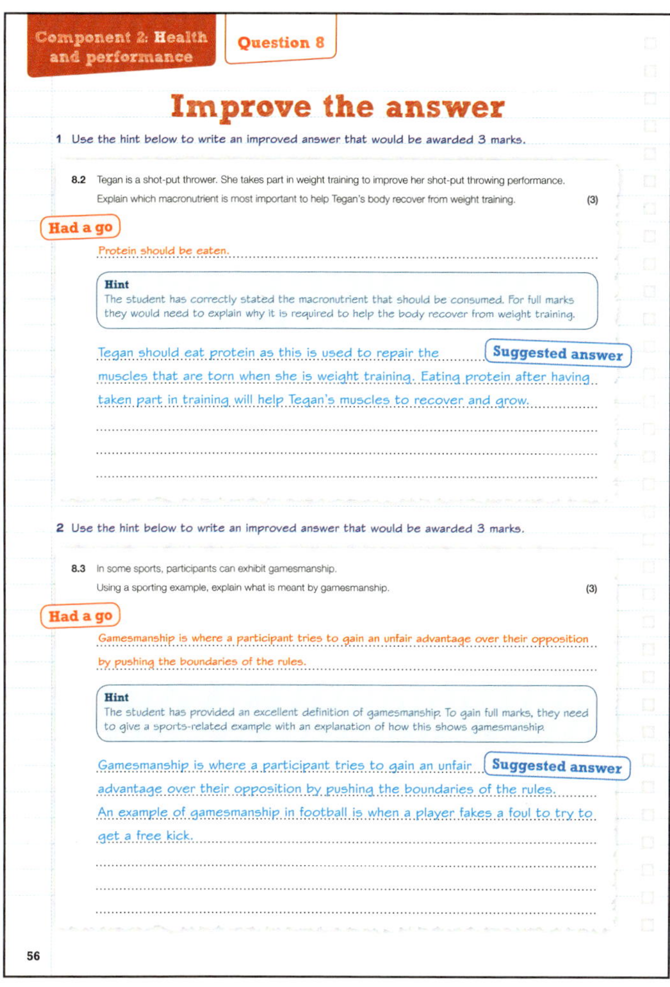

Improve the answer

1 Use the hint below to write an improved answer that would be awarded 3 marks.

8.2 Tegan is a shot-put thrower. She takes part in weight training to improve her shot-put throwing performance.

Explain which macronutrient is most important to help Tegan's body recover from weight training. (3)

Had a go

Protein should be eaten.

> **Hint**
> The student has correctly stated the macronutrient that should be consumed. For full marks they would need to explain why it is required to help the body recover from weight training.

Suggested answer

Tegan should eat protein as this is used to repair the muscles that are torn when she is weight training. Eating protein after having taken part in training will help Tegan's muscles to recover and grow.

2 Use the hint below to write an improved answer that would be awarded 3 marks.

8.3 In some sports, participants can exhibit gamesmanship.

Using a sporting example, explain what is meant by gamesmanship. (3)

Had a go

Gamesmanship is where a participant tries to gain an unfair advantage over their opposition by pushing the boundaries of the rules.

> **Hint**
> The student has provided an excellent definition of gamesmanship. To gain full marks, they need to give a sports-related example with an explanation of how this shows gamesmanship.

Suggested answer

Gamesmanship is where a participant tries to gain an unfair advantage over their opposition by pushing the boundaries of the rules. An example of gamesmanship in football is when a player fakes a foul to try to get a free kick.

56

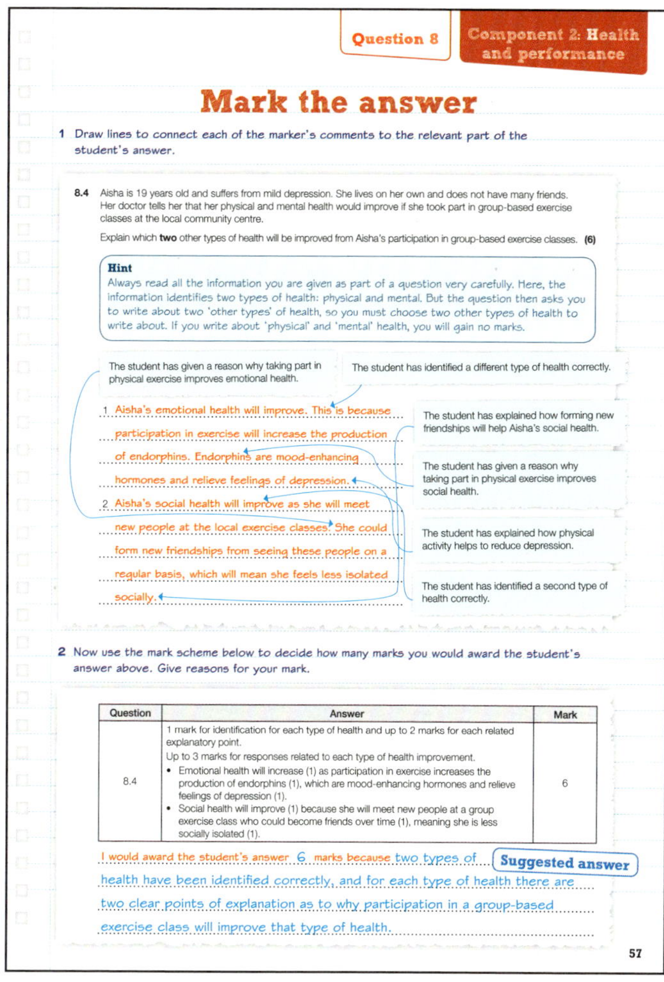

Mark the answer

1 Draw lines to connect each of the marker's comments to the relevant part of the student's answer.

8.4 Aisha is 19 years old and suffers from mild depression. She lives on her own and does not have many friends. Her doctor tells her that her physical and mental health would improve if she took part in group-based exercise classes at the local community centre.

Explain which **two** other types of health will be improved from Aisha's participation in group-based exercise classes. (6)

> **Hint**
> Always read all the information you are given as part of a question very carefully. Here, the information identifies two types of health: physical and mental. But the question then asks you to write about two 'other types' of health, so you must choose two other types of health to write about. If you write about 'physical' and 'mental' health, you will gain no marks.

The student has given a reason why taking part in physical exercise improves emotional health.

The student has identified a different type of health correctly.

1 Aisha's emotional health will improve. This is because participation in exercise will increase the production of endorphins. Endorphins are mood-enhancing hormones and relieve feelings of depression.

2 Aisha's social health will improve as she will meet new people at the local exercise classes. She could form new friendships from seeing these people on a regular basis, which will mean she feels less isolated socially.

The student has explained how forming new friendships will help Aisha's social health.

The student has given a reason why taking part in physical exercise improves social health.

The student has explained how physical activity helps to reduce depression.

The student has identified a second type of health correctly.

2 Now use the mark scheme below to decide how many marks you would award the student's answer above. Give reasons for your mark.

Question	Answer	Mark
8.4	1 mark for identification for each type of health and up to 2 marks for each related explanatory point. Up to 3 marks for responses related to each type of health improvement. • Emotional health will increase (1) as participation in exercise increases the production of endorphins (1), which are mood-enhancing hormones and relieve feelings of depression (1). • Social health will improve (1) because she will meet new people at a group exercise class who could become friends over time (1), meaning she is less socially isolated (1).	6

Suggested answer

I would award the student's answer 6 marks because two types of health have been identified correctly, and for each type of health there are two clear points of explanation as to why participation in a group-based exercise class will improve that type of health.

57

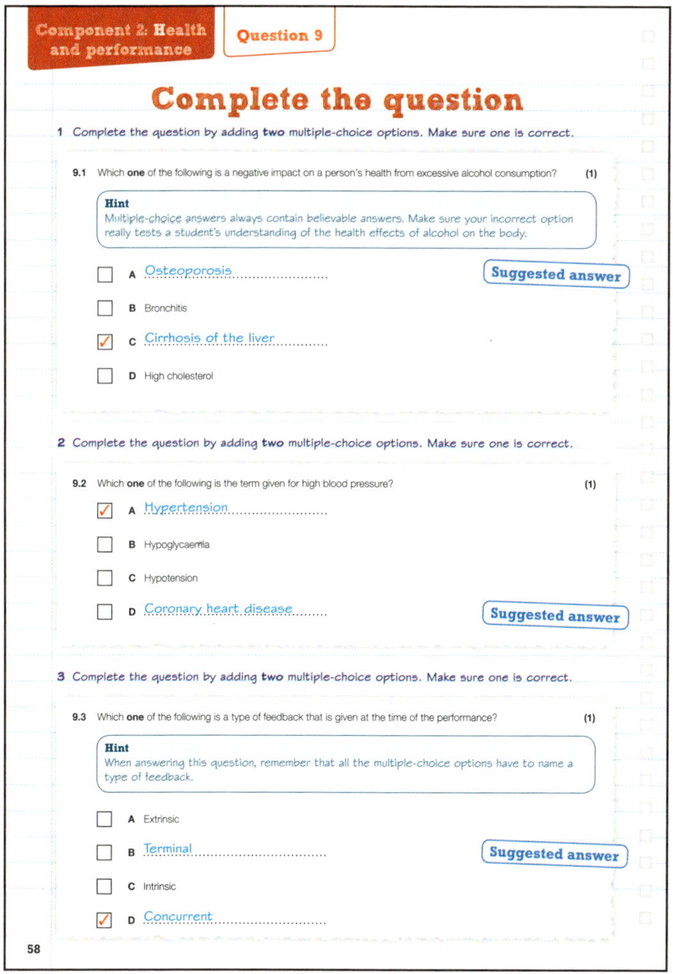

Complete the question

1 Complete the question by adding **two** multiple-choice options. Make sure one is correct.

9.1 Which **one** of the following is a negative impact on a person's health from excessive alcohol consumption? (1)

> **Hint**
> Multiple-choice answers always contain believable answers. Make sure your incorrect option really tests a student's understanding of the health effects of alcohol on the body.

☐ A Osteoporosis — **Suggested answer**

☐ B Bronchitis

☑ C Cirrhosis of the liver

☐ D High cholesterol

2 Complete the question by adding **two** multiple-choice options. Make sure one is correct.

9.2 Which **one** of the following is the term given for high blood pressure? (1)

☑ A Hypertension

☐ B Hypoglycaemia

☐ C Hypotension

☐ D Coronary heart disease — **Suggested answer**

3 Complete the question by adding **two** multiple-choice options. Make sure one is correct.

9.3 Which **one** of the following is a type of feedback that is given at the time of the performance? (1)

> **Hint**
> When answering this question, remember that all the multiple-choice options have to name a type of feedback.

☐ A Extrinsic

☐ B Terminal — **Suggested answer**

☐ C Intrinsic

☑ D Concurrent

58

Find the answer

1 Use the mark scheme below to find the student's answer that would be awarded 2 marks. Choose A, B or C. Explain your choice.

9.4 (a) Explain **one** advantage to a magazine company of using a well-known sports performer to advertise its new product. (2)

Question	Answer	Mark
9.4 (a)	1 mark for identification of an advantage and 1 mark for a related expansion. For example: • Using a well-known sports performer will increase awareness of the product (1) so more people are likely to buy the magazine, which will increase the company's profits (1). Accept any other appropriate responses.	2

(b) Explain **one** disadvantage to a magazine company of using a well-known sports performer to advertise its new product. (2)

Question	Answer	Mark
9.4 (b)	1 mark for identification of an advantage and 1 mark for each related expansion. • The sports performer may take part in inappropriate/illegal behaviour (1), which would make people not want to buy the magazine because it is associated with the performer's negative behaviour (1). Accept any other appropriate responses.	2

A
(a) It will make more people aware of the product, which will affect sales.
(b) The role model may be in the news, which would make people not want to buy the product.

B
(a) More people will be aware of the product so there is more chance that more people will buy it, so the company can make more money.
(b) The role model may take illegal recreational drugs, which would make people associate the magazine with that person's drug taking and stop them buying it.

C
(a) More people will know about the product as they will know the role model and think it must be a good product if they are advertising it.
(b) The role model may get worse at their sport so people would associate the magazine with playing poorly at sport.

Suggested answer

Answer B would be awarded 4 marks because for part (a) the student has identified an advantage (increased awareness of the product) and explained how this helps the magazine company (more people buy the magazine and the company makes more money).
For part (b) the student has identified a disadvantage (the magazine being associated with the performer's illegal drug taking) and explained how this could negatively affect the magazine (people will stop buying it).

59

Answers

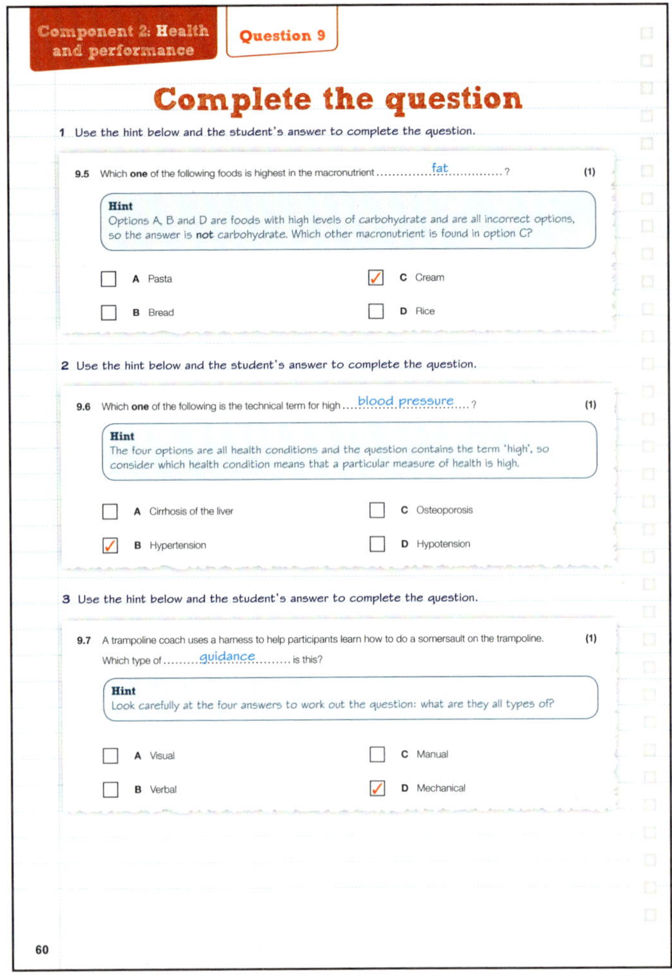

Complete the question

1 Use the hint below and the student's answer to complete the question.

9.5 Which **one** of the following foods is highest in the macronutrient .... fat ....? (1)

Hint
Options A, B and D are foods with high levels of carbohydrate and are all incorrect options, so the answer is **not** carbohydrate. Which other macronutrient is found in option C?

☐ **A** Pasta ☑ **C** Cream

☐ **B** Bread ☐ **D** Rice

2 Use the hint below and the student's answer to complete the question.

9.6 Which **one** of the following is the technical term for high ... blood pressure ...? (1)

Hint
The four options are all health conditions and the question contains the term 'high', so consider which health condition means that a particular measure of health is high.

☐ **A** Cirrhosis of the liver ☐ **C** Osteoporosis

☑ **B** Hypertension ☐ **D** Hypotension

3 Use the hint below and the student's answer to complete the question.

9.7 A trampoline coach uses a harness to help participants learn how to do a somersault on the trampoline. (1)
Which type of .... guidance .... is this?

Hint
Look carefully at the four answers to work out the question: what are they all types of?

☐ **A** Visual ☐ **C** Manual

☐ **B** Verbal ☑ **D** Mechanical

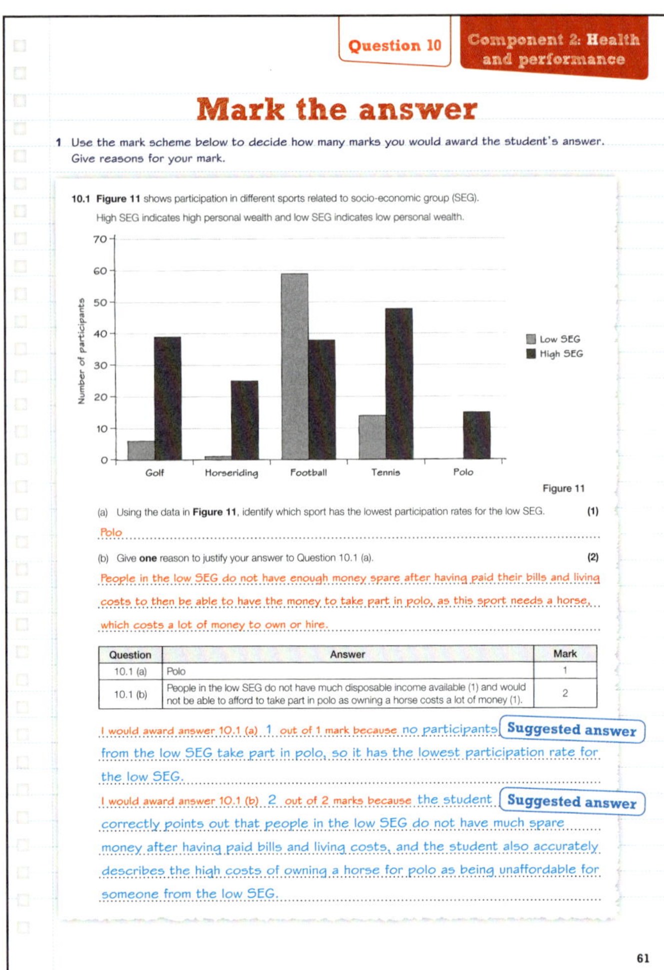

Mark the answer

1 Use the mark scheme below to decide how many marks you would award the student's answer. Give reasons for your mark.

10.1 **Figure 11** shows participation in different sports related to socio-economic group (SEG).
High SEG indicates high personal wealth and low SEG indicates low personal wealth.

(a) Using the data in **Figure 11**, identify which sport has the lowest participation rates for the low SEG. (1)
Polo

(b) Give **one** reason to justify your answer to Question 10.1 (a). (2)
People in the low SEG do not have enough money spare after having paid their bills and living costs to then be able to have the money to take part in polo, as this sport needs a horse, which costs a lot of money to own or hire.

Question	Answer	Mark
10.1 (a)	Polo	1
10.1 (b)	People in the low SEG do not have much disposable income available (1) and would not be able to afford to take part in polo as owning a horse costs a lot of money (1).	2

I would award answer 10.1 (a) 1 out of 1 mark because no participants **Suggested answer** from the low SEG take part in polo, so it has the lowest participation rate for the low SEG.

I would award answer 10.1 (b) 2 out of 2 marks because the student **Suggested answer** correctly points out that people in the low SEG do not have much spare money after having paid bills and living costs, and the student also accurately describes the high costs of owning a horse for polo as being unaffordable for someone from the low SEG.

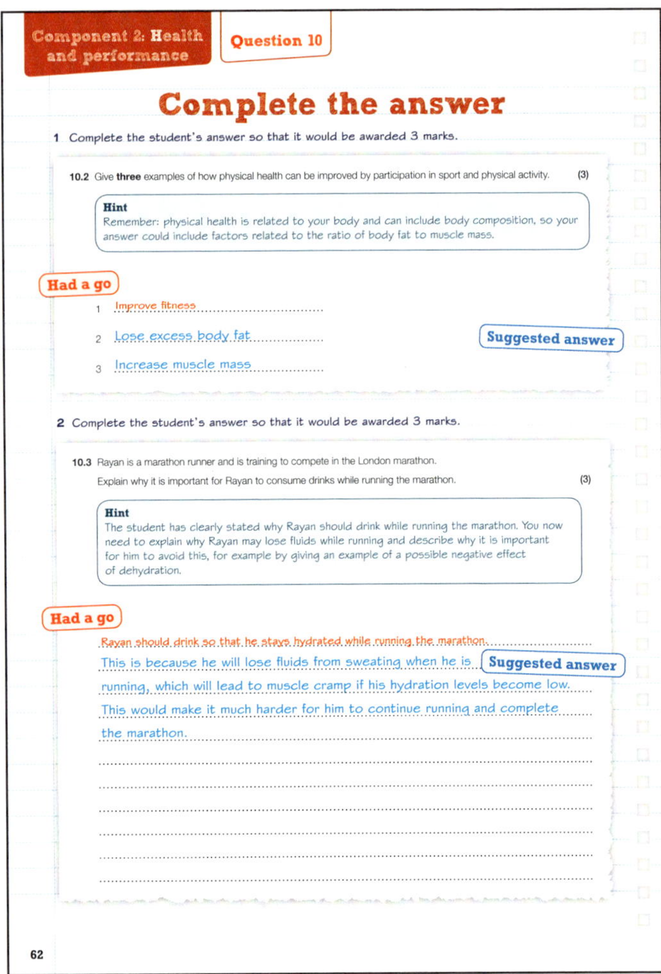

Complete the answer

1 Complete the student's answer so that it would be awarded 3 marks.

10.2 Give **three** examples of how physical health can be improved by participation in sport and physical activity. (3)

Hint
Remember: physical health is related to your body and can include body composition, so your answer could include factors related to the ratio of body fat to muscle mass.

Had a go

1 Improve fitness

2 Lose excess body fat **Suggested answer**

3 Increase muscle mass

2 Complete the student's answer so that it would be awarded 3 marks.

10.3 Rayan is a marathon runner and is training to compete in the London marathon.
Explain why it is important for Rayan to consume drinks while running the marathon. (3)

Hint
The student has clearly stated why Rayan should drink while running the marathon. You now need to explain why Rayan may lose fluids while running and describe why it is important for him to avoid this, for example by giving an example of a possible negative effect of dehydration.

Had a go

Rayan should drink so that he stays hydrated while running the marathon.
This is because he will lose fluids from sweating when he is **Suggested answer** running, which will lead to muscle cramp if his hydration levels become low. This would make it much harder for him to continue running and complete the marathon.

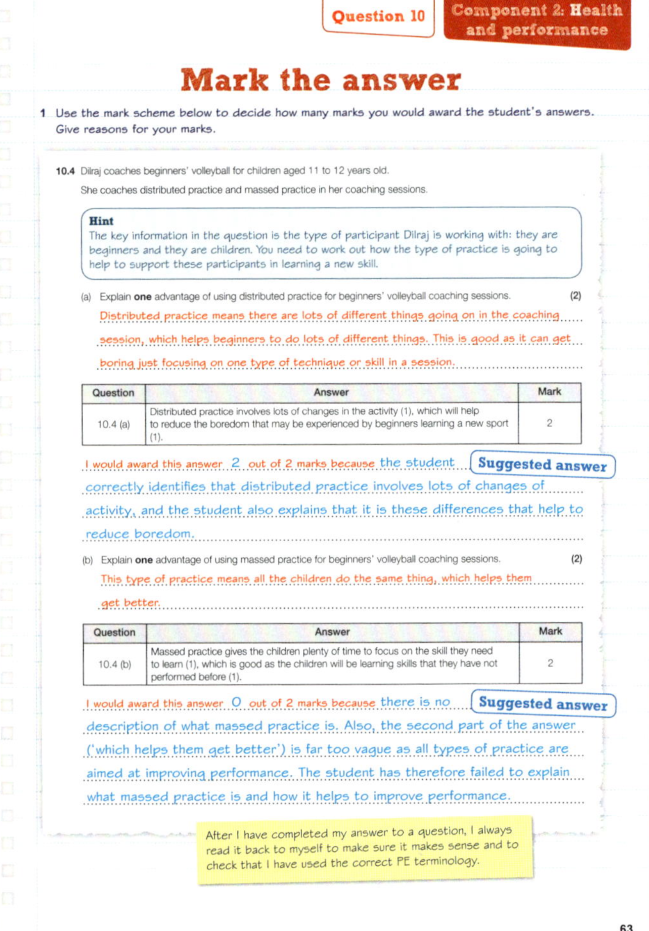

Mark the answer

1 Use the mark scheme below to decide how many marks you would award the student's answers. Give reasons for your marks.

10.4 Dilraj coaches beginners' volleyball for children aged 11 to 12 years old.
She coaches distributed practice and massed practice in her coaching sessions.

Hint
The key information in the question is the type of participant Dilraj is working with: they are beginners and they are children. You need to work out how the type of practice is going to help to support these participants in learning a new skill.

(a) Explain **one** advantage of using distributed practice for beginners' volleyball coaching sessions. (2)
Distributed practice means there are lots of different things going on in the coaching session, which helps beginners to do lots of different things. This is good as it can get boring just focusing on one type of technique or skill in a session.

Question	Answer	Mark
10.4 (a)	Distributed practice involves lots of changes in the activity (1), which will help to reduce the boredom that may be experienced by beginners learning a new sport (1).	2

I would award this answer 2 out of 2 marks because the student **Suggested answer** correctly identifies that distributed practice involves lots of changes of activity, and the student also explains that it is these differences that help to reduce boredom.

(b) Explain **one** advantage of using massed practice for beginners' volleyball coaching sessions. (2)
This type of practice means all the children do the same thing, which helps them get better.

Question	Answer	Mark
10.4 (b)	Massed practice gives the children plenty of time to focus on the skill they need to learn (1), which is good as the children will be learning skills that they have not performed before (1).	2

I would award this answer 0 out of 2 marks because there is no **Suggested answer** description of what massed practice is. Also, the second part of the answer ('which helps them get better') is far too vague as all types of practice are aimed at improving performance. The student has therefore failed to explain what massed practice is and how it helps to improve performance.

After I have completed my answer to a question, I always read it back to myself to make sure it makes sense and to check that I have used the correct PE terminology.

90

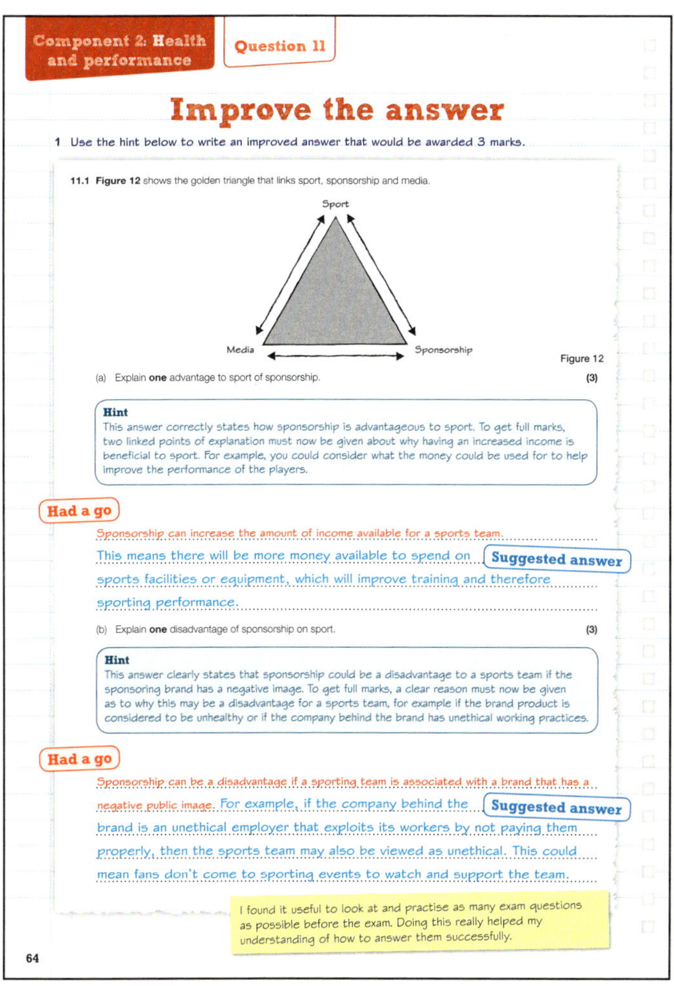

Component 2: Health and performance — Question 11

Improve the answer

1 Use the hint below to write an improved answer that would be awarded 3 marks.

11.1 **Figure 12** shows the golden triangle that links sport, sponsorship and media.

Figure 12

(a) Explain **one** advantage to sport of sponsorship. (3)

Hint
This answer correctly states how sponsorship is advantageous to sport. To get full marks, two linked points of explanation must now be given about why having an increased income is beneficial to sport. For example, you could consider what the money could be used for to help improve the performance of the players.

Had a go
Sponsorship can increase the amount of income available for a sports team. This means there will be more money available to spend on *[Suggested answer]* sports facilities or equipment, which will improve training and therefore sporting performance.

(b) Explain **one** disadvantage of sponsorship on sport. (3)

Hint
This answer clearly states that sponsorship could be a disadvantage to a sports team if the sponsoring brand has a negative image. To get full marks, a clear reason must now be given as to why this may be a disadvantage for a sports team, for example if the brand product is considered to be unhealthy or if the company behind the brand has unethical working practices.

Had a go
Sponsorship can be a disadvantage if a sporting team is associated with a brand that has a negative public image. For example, if the company behind the *[Suggested answer]* brand is an unethical employer that exploits its workers by not paying them properly, then the sports team may also be viewed as unethical. This could mean fans don't come to sporting events to watch and support the team.

> I found it useful to look at and practise as many exam questions as possible before the exam. Doing this really helped my understanding of how to answer them successfully.

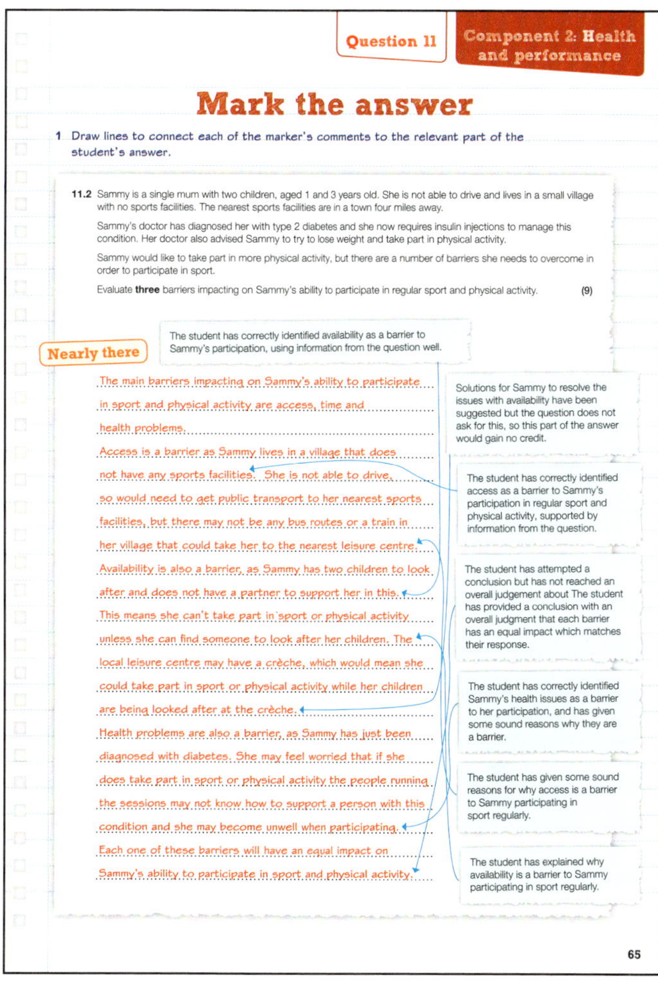

Question 11 — Component 2: Health and performance

Mark the answer

1 Draw lines to connect each of the marker's comments to the relevant part of the student's answer.

11.2 Sammy is a single mum with two children, aged 1 and 3 years old. She is not able to drive and lives in a small village with no sports facilities. The nearest sports facilities are in a town four miles away.

Sammy's doctor has diagnosed her with type 2 diabetes and she now requires insulin injections to manage this condition. Her doctor also advised Sammy to try to lose weight and take part in physical activity.

Sammy would like to take part in more physical activity, but there are a number of barriers she needs to overcome in order to participate in sport.

Evaluate **three** barriers impacting on Sammy's ability to participate in regular sport and physical activity. (9)

Nearly there

> The student has correctly identified availability as a barrier to Sammy's participation, using information from the question well.

The main barriers impacting on Sammy's ability to participate in sport and physical activity are access, time and health problems. Access is a barrier as Sammy lives in a village that does not have any sports facilities. She is not able to drive, so would need to get public transport to her nearest sports facilities, but there may not be any bus routes or a train in her village that could take her to the nearest leisure centre. Availability is also a barrier, as Sammy has two children to look after and does not have a partner to support her in this. This means she can't take part in sport or physical activity unless she can find someone to look after her children. The local leisure centre may have a crèche, which would mean she could take part in sport or physical activity while her children are being looked after at the crèche. Health problems are also a barrier, as Sammy has just been diagnosed with diabetes. She may feel worried that if she does take part in sport or physical activity the people running the sessions may not know how to support a person with this condition and she may become unwell when participating. Each one of these barriers will have an equal impact on Sammy's ability to participate in sport and physical activity.

Marker's comments:

- Solutions for Sammy to resolve the issues with availability have been suggested but the question does not ask for this, so this part of the answer would gain no credit.
- The student has correctly identified access as a barrier to Sammy's participation in regular sport and physical activity, supported by information from the question.
- The student has attempted a conclusion but has not reached an overall judgement about The student has provided a conclusion with an overall judgment that each barrier has an equal impact which matches their response.
- The student has correctly identified Sammy's health issues as a barrier to her participation, and has given some sound reasons why they are a barrier.
- The student has given some sound reasons for why access is a barrier to Sammy participating in sport regularly.
- The student has explained why availability is a barrier to Sammy participating in sport regularly.

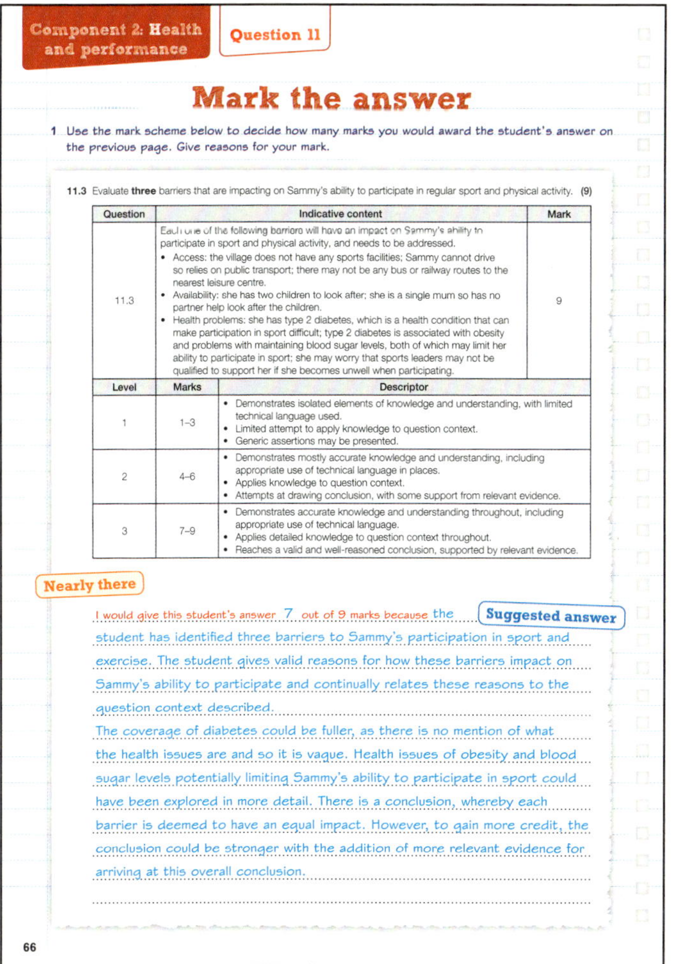

Component 2: Health and performance — Question 11

Mark the answer

1 Use the mark scheme below to decide how many marks you would award the student's answer on the previous page. Give reasons for your mark.

11.3 Evaluate **three** barriers that are impacting on Sammy's ability to participate in regular sport and physical activity. (9)

Question	Indicative content	Mark
11.3	Each one of the following barriers will have an impact on Sammy's ability to participate in sport and physical activity, and needs to be addressed. • Access: the village does not have any sports facilities; Sammy cannot drive so relies on public transport; there may not be any bus or railway routes to the nearest leisure centre. • Availability: she has two children to look after; she is a single mum so has no partner help look after the children. • Health problems: she has type 2 diabetes, which is a health condition that can make participation in sport difficult; type 2 diabetes is associated with obesity and problems with maintaining blood sugar levels, both of which may limit her ability to participate in sport; she may worry that sports leaders may not be qualified to support her if she becomes unwell when participating.	9

Level	Marks	Descriptor
1	1–3	• Demonstrates isolated elements of knowledge and understanding, with limited technical language used. • Limited attempt to apply knowledge to question context. • Generic assertions may be presented.
2	4–6	• Demonstrates mostly accurate knowledge and understanding, including appropriate use of technical language in places. • Applies knowledge to question context. • Attempts at drawing conclusion, with some support from relevant evidence.
3	7–9	• Demonstrates accurate knowledge and understanding throughout, including appropriate use of technical language. • Applies detailed knowledge to question context throughout. • Reaches a valid and well-reasoned conclusion, supported by relevant evidence.

Nearly there

[Suggested answer]
I would give this student's answer 7 out of 9 marks because the student has identified three barriers to Sammy's participation in sport and exercise. The student gives valid reasons for how these barriers impact on Sammy's ability to participate and continually relates these reasons to the question context described.

The coverage of diabetes could be fuller, as there is no mention of what the health issues are and so it is vague. Health issues of obesity and blood sugar levels potentially limiting Sammy's ability to participate in sport could have been explored in more detail. There is a conclusion, whereby each barrier is deemed to have an equal impact. However, to gain more credit, the conclusion could be stronger with the addition of more relevant evidence for arriving at this overall conclusion.

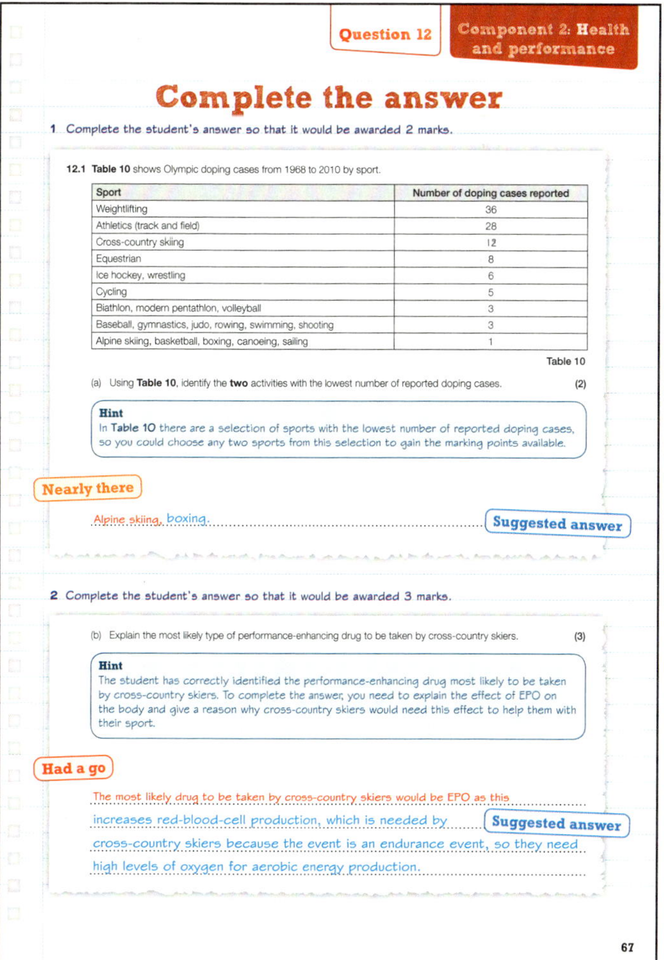

Question 12 — Component 2: Health and performance

Complete the answer

1 Complete the student's answer so that it would be awarded 2 marks.

12.1 **Table 10** shows Olympic doping cases from 1968 to 2010 by sport.

Sport	Number of doping cases reported
Weightlifting	36
Athletics (track and field)	28
Cross-country skiing	12
Equestrian	8
Ice hockey, wrestling	6
Cycling	5
Biathlon, modern pentathlon, volleyball	3
Baseball, gymnastics, judo, rowing, swimming, shooting	3
Alpine skiing, basketball, boxing, canoeing, sailing	1

Table 10

(a) Using **Table 10**, identify the **two** activities with the lowest number of reported doping cases. (2)

Hint
In **Table 10** there are a selection of sports with the lowest number of reported doping cases, so you could choose any two sports from this selection to gain the marking points available.

Nearly there

Alpine skiing, boxing. *[Suggested answer]*

2 Complete the student's answer so that it would be awarded 3 marks.

(b) Explain the most likely type of performance-enhancing drug to be taken by cross-country skiers. (3)

Hint
The student has correctly identified the performance-enhancing drug most likely to be taken by cross-country skiers. To complete the answer, you need to explain the effect of EPO on the body and give a reason why cross-country skiers would need this effect to help them with their sport.

Had a go
The most likely drug to be taken by cross-country skiers would be EPO as this increases red-blood-cell production, which is needed by *[Suggested answer]* cross-country skiers because the event is an endurance event, so they need high levels of oxygen for aerobic energy production.

Answers

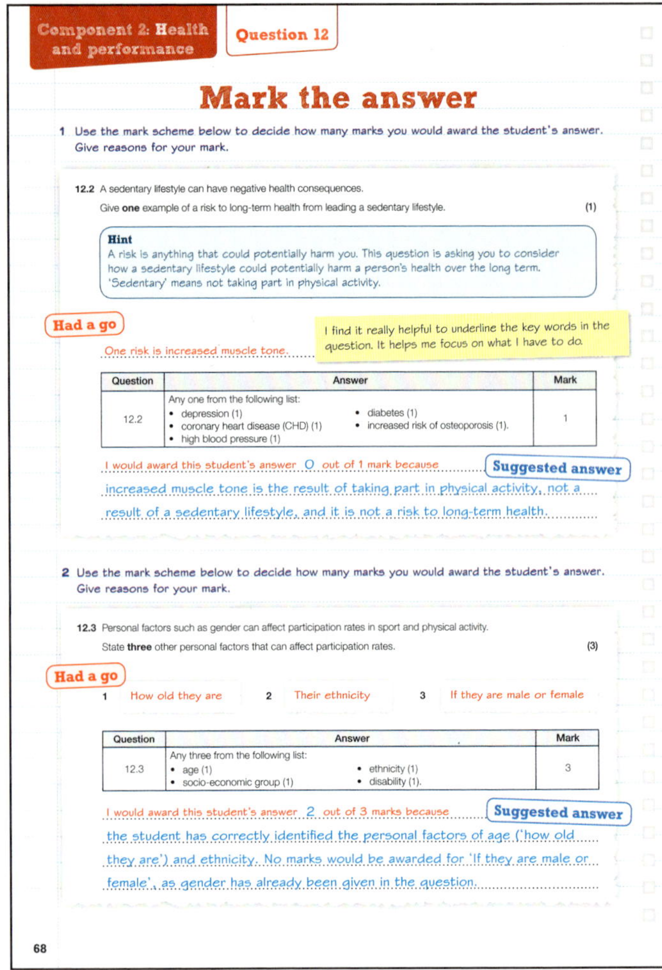

Component 2: Health and performance | Question 12

Mark the answer

1 Use the mark scheme below to decide how many marks you would award the student's answer. Give reasons for your mark.

12.2 A sedentary lifestyle can have negative health consequences.

Give **one** example of a risk to long-term health from leading a sedentary lifestyle. (1)

Hint
A risk is anything that could potentially harm you. This question is asking you to consider how a sedentary lifestyle could potentially harm a person's health over the long term. 'Sedentary' means not taking part in physical activity.

Had a go

One risk is increased muscle tone.

I find it really helpful to underline the key words in the question. It helps me focus on what I have to do.

Question	Answer	Mark
12.2	Any one from the following list: • depression (1) • coronary heart disease (CHD) (1) • high blood pressure (1) • diabetes (1) • increased risk of osteoporosis (1).	1

I would award this student's answer O out of 1 mark because increased muscle tone is the result of taking part in physical activity, not a result of a sedentary lifestyle, and it is not a risk to long-term health.

Suggested answer

2 Use the mark scheme below to decide how many marks you would award the student's answer. Give reasons for your mark.

12.3 Personal factors such as gender can affect participation rates in sport and physical activity.

State **three** other personal factors that can affect participation rates. (3)

Had a go

1 How old they are   2 Their ethnicity   3 If they are male or female

Question	Answer	Mark
12.3	Any three from the following list: • age (1) • socio-economic group (1) • ethnicity (1) • disability (1).	3

I would award this student's answer 2 out of 3 marks because the student has correctly identified the personal factors of age ('how old they are') and ethnicity. No marks would be awarded for 'If they are male or female', as gender has already been given in the question.

Suggested answer

68

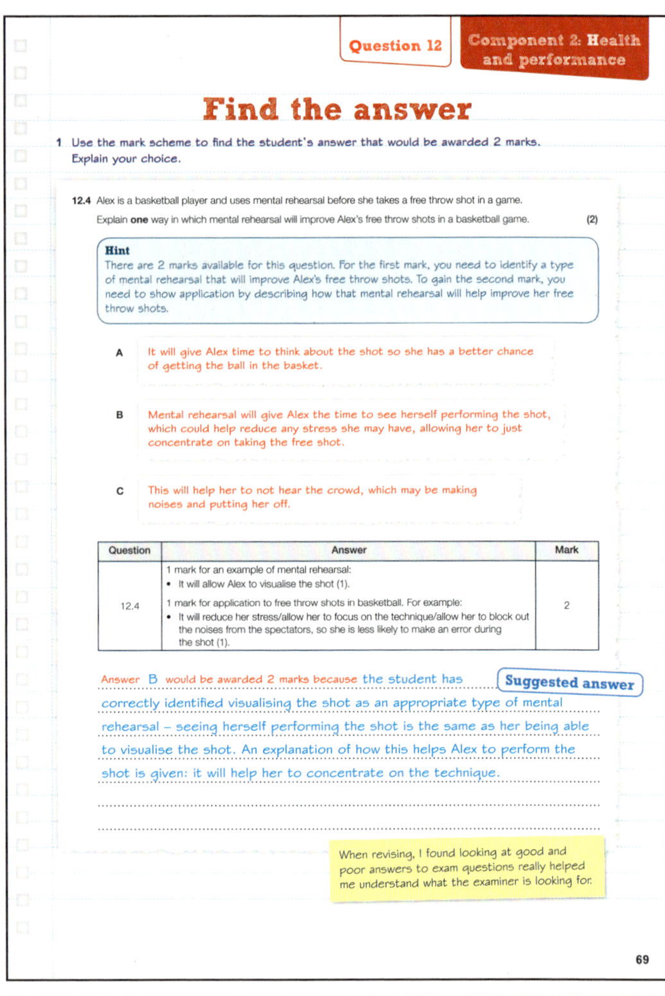

Question 12 | Component 2: Health and performance

Find the answer

1 Use the mark scheme to find the student's answer that would be awarded 2 marks. Explain your choice.

12.4 Alex is a basketball player and uses mental rehearsal before she takes a free throw shot in a game.

Explain **one** way in which mental rehearsal will improve Alex's free throw shots in a basketball game. (2)

Hint
There are 2 marks available for this question. For the first mark, you need to identify a type of mental rehearsal that will improve Alex's free throw shots. To gain the second mark, you need to show application by describing how that mental rehearsal will help improve her free throw shots.

A It will give Alex time to think about the shot so she has a better chance of getting the ball in the basket.

B Mental rehearsal will give Alex the time to see herself performing the shot, which could help reduce any stress she may have, allowing her to just concentrate on taking the free shot.

C This will help her to not hear the crowd, which may be making noises and putting her off.

Question	Answer	Mark
12.4	1 mark for an example of mental rehearsal: • It will allow Alex to visualise the shot (1). 1 mark for application to free throw shots in basketball. For example: • It will reduce her stress/allow her to focus on the technique/allow her to block out the noises from the spectators, so she is less likely to make an error during the shot (1).	2

Answer B would be awarded 2 marks because the student has correctly identified visualising the shot as an appropriate type of mental rehearsal – seeing herself performing the shot is the same as her being able to visualise the shot. An explanation of how this helps Alex to perform the shot is given: it will help her to concentrate on the technique.

Suggested answer

When revising, I found looking at good and poor answers to exam questions really helped me understand what the examiner is looking for.

69

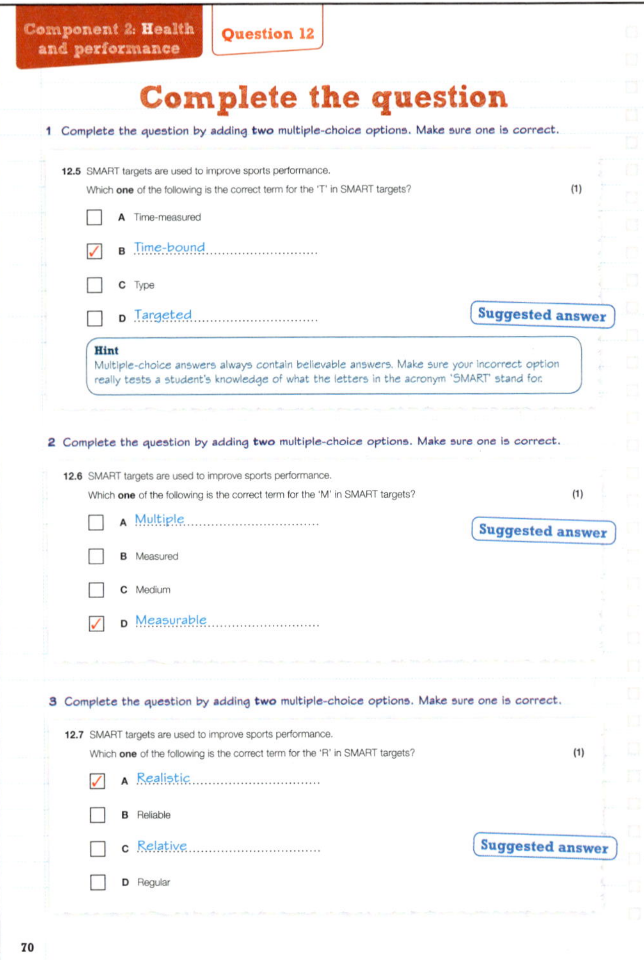

Component 2: Health and performance | Question 12

Complete the question

1 Complete the question by adding **two** multiple-choice options. Make sure one is correct.

12.5 SMART targets are used to improve sports performance.

Which **one** of the following is the correct term for the 'T' in SMART targets? (1)

A Time-measured
✓ B Time-bound
C Type
D Targeted

Suggested answer

Hint
Multiple-choice answers always contain believable answers. Make sure your incorrect option really tests a student's knowledge of what the letters in the acronym 'SMART' stand for.

2 Complete the question by adding **two** multiple-choice options. Make sure one is correct.

12.6 SMART targets are used to improve sports performance.

Which **one** of the following is the correct term for the 'M' in SMART targets? (1)

A Multiple
B Measured
C Medium
✓ D Measurable

Suggested answer

3 Complete the question by adding **two** multiple-choice options. Make sure one is correct.

12.7 SMART targets are used to improve sports performance.

Which **one** of the following is the correct term for the 'R' in SMART targets? (1)

✓ A Realistic
B Reliable
C Relative
D Regular

Suggested answer

70

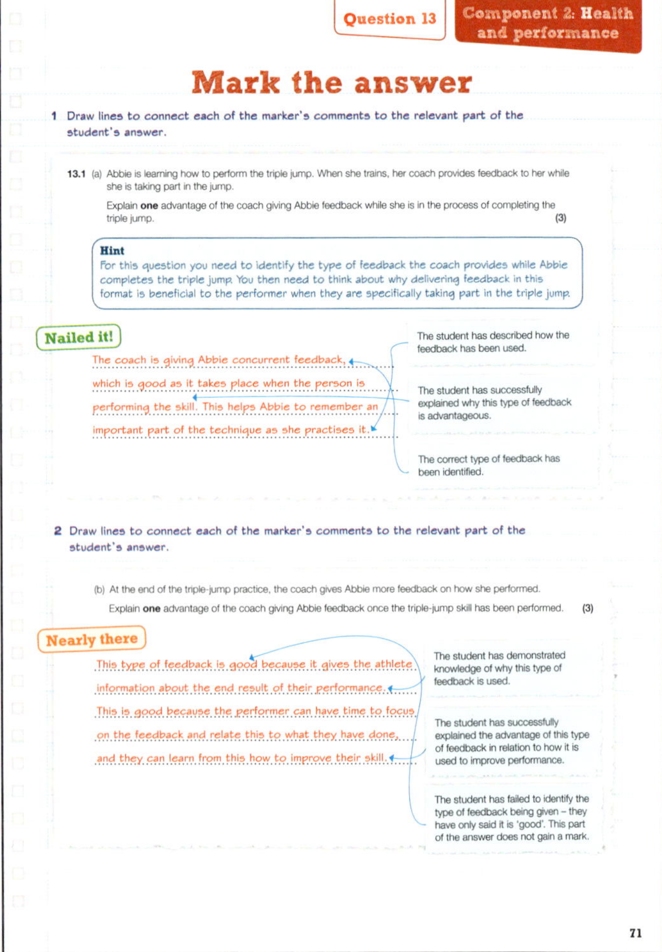

Question 13 | Component 2: Health and performance

Mark the answer

1 Draw lines to connect each of the marker's comments to the relevant part of the student's answer.

13.1 (a) Abbie is learning how to perform the triple jump. When she trains, her coach provides feedback to her while she is taking part in the jump.

Explain **one** advantage of the coach giving Abbie feedback while she is in the process of completing the triple jump. (3)

Hint
For this question you need to identify the type of feedback the coach provides while Abbie completes the triple jump. You then need to think about why delivering feedback in this format is beneficial to the performer when they are specifically taking part in the triple jump.

Nailed it!

The coach is giving Abbie concurrent feedback, which is good as it takes place when the person is performing the skill. This helps Abbie to remember an important part of the technique as she practises it.

The student has described how the feedback has been used.

The student has successfully explained why this type of feedback is advantageous.

The correct type of feedback has been identified.

2 Draw lines to connect each of the marker's comments to the relevant part of the student's answer.

(b) At the end of the triple-jump practice, the coach gives Abbie more feedback on how she performed.

Explain **one** advantage of the coach giving Abbie feedback once the triple-jump skill has been performed. (3)

Nearly there

This type of feedback is good because it gives the athlete information about the end result of their performance. This is good because the performer can have time to focus on the feedback and relate this to what they have done, and they can learn from this how to improve their skill.

The student has demonstrated knowledge of why this type of feedback is used.

The student has successfully explained the advantage of this type of feedback in relation to how it is used to improve performance.

The student has failed to identify the type of feedback being given – they have only said it is 'good'. This part of the answer does not gain a mark.

71